The Definitive Guide to Underwriting Multifamily Acquisitions

Develop the skills to confidently analyze and invest in multifamily real estate

ROBERT BEARDSLEY

ISBN-13: 979-8-6296-7739-0

PRAISE FOR
THE DEFINITIVE GUIDE TO
UNDERWRITING MULTIFAMILY
ACQUISITIONS

"This is a phenomenal resource for understanding how to underwrite a multifamily deal. Our group, PassiveInvesting.com, has been using a variation of Rob's underwriting model for a couple of years now and we have acquired over $220mil+ in multifamily assets. I highly recommend you listening to Rob and taking advantage of knowledge within this book."

–Dan Handford, Managing Partner with
PassiveInvesting.com

"The Definitive Guide to Underwriting Multifamily Acquisitions is a must-read for both passive investors and sponsors looking to take their investments to the next level. Rob delivers lesser-known insights regarding sensitivity analyses, stress tests, and partnership structures in a concise format. Rob provides readers the tools to make confident investments in multifamily partnerships/syndications."

–Joe Fairless, Co-Founder of Ashcroft Capital

"Rob Beardsley is a true expert at the all-important but often ignored art and science of underwriting. The Definitive guide is a fantastic resource for anyone that needs to learn more about underwriting, and even professional underwriters will find plenty of food for thought in here."

–Neal Bawa, CEO, Grocapitus and MultifamilyU

"The Definitive Guide to Underwriting Multifamily Acquisitions is a zero-fluff approach to analyzing potential apartment acquisitions. Not only does Rob tell you the exact metrics to focus on prior to moving forward with a purchase, he also gives you dozens of rules of thumb that you can refer back to when underwriting a new opportunity. This alone will save you countless hours while sifting through deals, trying to find the diamond in the rough, and removing those without potential."

–Hunter Thompson, author of Raising Capital for Real Estate & Founder of Asym Capital

"I've had the pleasure of knowing Rob as a syndicator and investor in the multifamily niche. He's supported reviews on several of our projects. I've always been impressed by Rob's attention to details, ease of explaining more complicated concepts and fresh perspective on deal structuring. I expect you will find this book highly useful as I did."

–David Thompson, CEO and Founder, Thompson Investing

CONTENTS

INTRODUCTION

"We suffer from knowing the numbers" —*Sam Zell*

I wrote this book because I wish it had existed when I first began learning to underwrite multifamily acquisitions and building my own underwriting model. Additionally, over the last few years, many people have reached out to me asking for the best resources to learn the nuances of underwriting as well as how to build an underwriting model from scratch themselves. I struggled to provide strong recommendations. While I learned from experience and wide-ranging research, there were few resources that I could confidently suggest. Instead, I invited them to read my articles on the subject in the meantime, and to stay tuned for an upcoming book from yours truly. I'm excited to finally share this book with you and to finally deliver a resource for those seeking a firmer grasp of the numbers that drive projected returns in multifamily investments.

It may seem strange to you that a book about such a vital skill of the real estate investment business has never been written before. I believe there is some level of lack of transparency that most investors prefer to have about their valuation process, rather than open up their methods to scrutiny. Additionally, some may want to espouse the myth that there is some secret sauce or rare ability required to understand valuation. I don't believe this to be true. I think pretty much anyone can become proficient in underwriting with a fair amount of effort and the right guidance, which is why I wrote this book. I endeavored to include in this book a good balance of introductory explanations alongside some more complex topics.

The ability to break a deal down into its numerical components is a tremendously important and often neglected skill. All too often, passive investors make investment decisions based solely on a sponsor's track record or shiny pitch deck. Being able to confidently project returns across different geographies, business plans, financing structures and hold periods empowers an investor (whether active or passive) to identify and pursue opportunities that stand out above others. For sponsors, this is essential; underwriting is most likely a daily part of their acquisitions pipeline. However, limited partners, especially retail investors, may not be in the habit of underwriting deals on a daily basis, and may have no frame of reference as to how the average deal "pencils" in a market or at a particular point in the market cycle. Some newer investors may have never even underwritten a single deal before! If that's you, fear not! That is what I'd like to change with this book – by providing the knowledge and tools investors need to build and interpret pro formas and sensitivity analyses. If you're more experienced, hopefully you can gain some additional insights or refinements to your process by taking a peek at ours.

One final motivation for writing this book is the small hope that I could convince investors to underwrite just a little more realistically (conservatively), which would reduce the number of deals getting bid up based on rosy assumptions. If we could, together as investors, choose to underwrite with slightly different mechanics and assumptions, we could potentially create a healthier market for everyone with higher returns and safer risk/return trade-offs. Perhaps it's unlikely, but wouldn't that be something?

What is Underwriting and Why is it Important?

"Success in investing doesn't come from buying good things, but from buying things well, and it's essential to know the difference. It's not a matter of what you buy, but what you pay for it." –Howard Marks

Underwriting is the process of collecting and organizing the financial information needed to build a projection of income, expenses, and investment returns (a pro forma). These projections guide investment decisions related to purchase, refinance, and sale. It also impacts potential choices of GP/LP partnership structure or more complex financing structures such as mezzanine debt or preferred equity. Lastly, underwriting can be used to create sensitivity analyses, which help to evaluate investment decisions in light of possible upside/downside scenarios. As a real estate investor, the value of the asset boils down to just the numbers – pricing and returns – not how pretty the landscaping looks. The goal of underwriting is to estimate these key assumptions with as much clarity and confidence as possible. This value and pricing-focused mode of decision making is far more likely to achieve good results compared to deciding to invest in a property because it is in a good location, is in good condition, or has high median household incomes within a 1-mile radius. While those factors are extremely important and must be taken into account, they do not by themselves make a good investment if the price for the asset is too rich. Remember, it's not how good the thing is that you buy, it's how well you buy it. Price and quality are inextricably tied.

Underwriting saves us from making foolhardy decisions that ignore pricing – the lackluster returns will be staring right back at us in the model. Instead of making decisions based on a scattershot approach or a context-free checklist – "Population growth? Check. Low crime? Check. Strong rent and sales comparables? Check…" – comprehensive underwriting lets us translate qualitative data into numbers and distill all of these factors into a "bottom line" using an appropriate pricing and risk model. The key function of underwriting is to derive a price for an asset that makes sense for us/our investors, based on our specific target returns and risk tolerance. However, target returns cannot and should not be developed in a vacuum. Target returns need to be based on feedback provided by the market, which can only be determined by underwriting and bidding on countless opportunities in order to identify the average prospective returns for various markets and investment types (core-plus, value-add, opportunistic). Then you can determine where you want your target returns to be in relation to the average returns available in that given market.

Use too high a return target, and price targets will be too low – nobody will sell and we will remain theoretical "investors," having made no investments. Too low a return target, and we will achieve low returns at best and quite possibly even lose money.

This, of course, proceeds from your pre-existing market/asset thesis, such as investing in luxury apartments in San Jose, CA due to Silicon Valley's strength and resiliency as a world class labor market of young professional renters. Once you have made this decision, you can begin to analyze deals in the market and begin to see what the average returns available in that market are as well as compare the average market opportunity between various markets. For some, the choice of market may come down to proximity; others may look further afield based on demographics, economics, and market trends.

For example, in San Jose, despite strong future outlook and demand drivers, prospective returns are low because all investors can see these demand drivers and have bid up prices accordingly. Since San Jose is perceived as low-risk, investors are willing to accept lower returns still. Although Oklahoma City may be a worse market than San Jose in terms of incomes, economics, and market prospects, better investments can still be made in Oklahoma City if the pricing relative to those prospects is more attractive than San Jose's pricing relative to its prospects. Comprehensive underwriting is the one tool that allows us to compare different investments on equal footing, and determine what risk or future growth expectations are implied by an investment's pricing. From there, we can decide whether we are comfortable with the growth and operational assumptions that our projected investment returns depend on – taking into account the assumptions baked into market prices. The "best" markets may not be the best value or the best investment. We personally aren't big fans of either San Jose or Oklahoma City as we prefer to operate in markets that are somewhere in between those in terms of size and growth prospects.

Which Underwriting Model to Use/Building Your Own

"Garbage in, garbage out. Or rather more felicitously: the tree of nonsense is watered with error, and from its branches swing the pumpkins of disaster." –Nick Harkaway

It is extremely valuable from both a pedagogical and real-world application perspective to build your own underwriting model. The process of creating your own model forces you to learn every calculation and step in the process and better understand how each assumption works with the others in the model. All models are built differently and sometimes there is no right or wrong formula, so it is helpful to use a model you built, which you intimately know how all of its formulas work.

While building a model from scratch is outside the scope of this book, I'll offer a few thoughts on the matter for readers who want to get their hands dirty. The best way to get started is by downloading and playing with as many models as you can get your hands on. This will allow you to see various styles and formats as well as see the more common ways certain calculations are made.

It is also helpful to underwrite the same deal through all of the models you downloaded to see the variation in the resulting outputs even when using the same exact numbers. Even some minor differences in calculation methods can vary projected returns substantially. Put simply, I could take the exact same numbers (rents, expenses, vacancy, exit cap rate, rent growth, etc.) and get a 15% IRR with one model and a 20% IRR with another. Neither IRR is necessarily more correct (I would most likely lean towards the 15% though). The specific output is less important than YOU understanding and trusting the output.

Once you have become familiar with a handful of models, you can begin to take them apart and put them back together, tweaking a few things along the way. Then you can take the best aspects of these models and incorporate them into your new model, which will certainly evolve over time as you underwrite more deals and come across new scenarios. Be sure that whichever model you choose to work with has monthly pro forma calculations. Annual calculations can be overly simplified or error-prone. Our model calculates everything on a monthly basis and simply adds up the months to create an annual cash flow pro forma that is easy to read and understand.

Whether building your own model or using someone else's, consistency is key. Throughout this book, we will reference our internal Lone Star Capital underwriting model, which I spent hundreds of hours building and rebuilding from scratch.

For the purposes of following along in this book, I highly recommend heading to www.lscre.com and clicking the link at the top to get your copy of our underwriting model.

You will develop confidence in a model, even if it

isn't yours, by putting 100+ deals through it so that you get to know the typical model outputs based on various scenarios. Please follow the link above to receive our Underwriting Model Package Dropbox link which includes our latest and greatest underwriting model as well as video tutorials and examples.

KEEPING IT SIMPLE

©2004 Scott Adams, Inc

Before we dive into the full underwriting process, if you're a passive investor and lack the time or inclination to dive into an exhaustive analysis of the viability/strength of proposed investments, here are the three key, high-level points I recommend focusing on:

1. Sponsor: Team and Experience
2. Deal Structure: Alignment of Interest, Fees, and Sponsor Co-Invest

3. Deal: Rent Growth, Exit Cap Rate, and Yield on Cost

Point #1 – Sponsor: Team and Experience

People often say a great deal cannot make up for a bad sponsor. If you're quickly evaluating an investment, focus on the sponsor's team and experience. It is important to understand how the sponsor property manages and asset manages its portfolio. The best way to learn more about this is by researching or inquiring about current and previous investments.

Don't be satisfied with just a track record of completed investments since this can be missing the full picture. Sponsors often include deals in their track record in which they don't or didn't have operational involvement in; this doesn't really provide insight into their asset management capabilities. Further, the sponsor may have unrealized investments (not yet sold) which are underperforming, which is why it is helpful to evaluate current and exited deals.

The best evidence of strong management are case studies which compare the underwriting performed at acquisition and the actual financial results of the investment. Looking at case studies with this added level of scrutiny, can help uncover if a few strong return deals are a function of above-average rent growth or price appreciation (lower exit cap rate) rather than from expertise and execution.

It is essential that the passive investor understand how the sponsor plans to manage the proposed investment and incorporate it into their existing portfolio. A real estate private equity firm or asset manager can either manage investments in-house via an affiliated management arm, or they can hire a third-party property management company. Countless companies using either approach have achieved success, so there is no right answer. However, generally speaking, vertically integrated owner-operators like Lone Star Capital can exercise tighter control over operations and thus better align day-to-day property management with ownership goals.

The reason for this is third-party property management companies are compensated via a management fee, typically 3% of gross revenues. This isn't huge to begin with, and it's far from pure profit – management companies bear many expenses as part of the work they do to earn that fee. Further, management companies face an imperfect set of incentives.

Owners benefit most by maximizing profit – both by raising revenue (rent, occupancy) *as much as possible* and by reducing expenses *as much as possible*. Take occupancy – expenses increase less for each marginal occupant, and so the marginal tenant is the most profitable. For managers, a property that easily achieves 90% occupancy may require close attention to reach 95% occupancy, while earning only a tiny bit more income – attention that could be spent managing another property all together! So long as they perform well *enough* to keep their contracts, far better to have two properties at 90% occupancy than one property at 95% for a third-party management company.

If managers have little incentive to maximize occupancy and revenue – the top half of the profit equation – they have precisely zero financial incentive to minimize expenses (whether "above the line" operating expenses or "below the line" capex or unit renovations). Since they are compensated on revenue rather than profit, they earn exactly the same no matter what the costs, as long as they don't get fired.

Once we have answered questions like, "who manages the properties, and what is their local presence?", we can begin to understand more about how a new acquisition will fit in the owner's and/or manager's portfolio. Will they need to add corporate staff such as a regional manager or an additional accountant? Does the sponsor have a dedicated asset management team already in place for this project, or will the sponsor need to bring on additional talent? While less often discussed than location, cash yield, or internal rate of return, property management is *the* essential factor that makes projected returns a reality in multifamily investments.

Another important factor to consider about a sponsor is their accounting and reporting. Firstly, robust accounting and reporting allows a sponsor to glean actionable insights from the data to add value to the investment. Additionally, quality reporting is important for LP investors interested in transparency and to gauge the progress of the investment.

Point #2 – Deal Structure: Alignment of Interest, Fees, and Sponsor Co-Invest

We will go in much further depth about deal/partnership structures later in this book, but the most important points are alignment of interests, fees, and sponsor co-invest. For passive investors, an investment's structure should align interests between sponsor and investors and be reasonable from a fee and profit split perspective. This means that the structure puts investors first via a preferred return (preferably an IRR hurdle – meaning a sponsor's performance compensation is subordinate to a full return of capital to investors).

An even more powerful aligner of interests is cash invested by the sponsor alongside investors at the same terms. The co-investment amount should be meaningful in relation to the sponsor's net worth/ability to invest in the project net of fees being received.

Fees, of course, should also be a consideration; we will later discuss typical investment fees, as well as possible hidden fees.

Point #3 – Deal: Rent Growth, Exit Cap Rate, and Yield on Cost

The passive investor's active role ends once capital is committed – thus investment decision-making is essential. Can you assess the quality of the proposed investment at a high level, by evaluating the prospective returns against the risks of the project? Of course, the formal way to do this is via a full underwriting – forecasting cash flows for a three to ten-year period, along with a reversion value (what happens when you sell the investment). However, a few questions and key metrics can help cut through the noise without having to go through a full underwriting process, saving time and maximizing deal flow.

It is always helpful to request the sponsor's internal underwriting model. First, it is important to see how they are deriving their projections. Second, we can evaluate how sophisticated it is. Sophistication isn't everything, of course. I've seen very complex models that outputted bogus numbers ("garbage in, garbage out"). Lastly, sometimes sponsors are reluctant to share their internal model... in which case, my advice is to run! Who knows what they're hiding. There is no good reason to keep underwriting a secret. Everyone in the industry is using more or less the same formulas – what varies is the inputs they plug in to them. Certainly, there's no "magic" in the underwriting that makes investments work better. In the end the property generally goes to whoever pays the most; no magic in anyone's model can change that.

With the sponsor's model in hand, look for the key inputs of rent growth and terminal (exit) cap rate. If you can't find the rent growth input, look at the year over year change in revenue in the penultimate and final years of the cash flow projections (earlier years are often affected by the value-add plan, such as raising rents). These last two years should show just the baseline rent increase projected in the model. This is typically 2% and should never exceed 3%.

Terminal (exit) cap should be identifiable, or it can be calculated by dividing the sale year NOI divided by the projected sale price. Exit cap should be 50–100bps above the area's current market cap rate. If you are unsure what the prevailing market cap rates are, consult the sponsor and other credible sources such as local investors and brokers. Projected cashflow from sale, in the final period of the investment, is by far the largest single component of the NPV/IRR calculation, since sale price equals the final year's income divided by terminal cap rate. Thus, income growth, compounded through the final year, and the cap rate at which that final year income is valued by have an outsized effect on the projected returns of the investment.

Next, check the operating expenses. Even without knowledge of operating expenses or multifamily property management, we can compare historical expenses (trailing 12 months of expenses) incurred by the previous owner with the projected future expenses. If the difference is substantial, ask why – given the explanation, we can decide for ourselves whether the projections are realistic.

Lastly, use the projected rent and expenses to calculate the investment's projected yield on cost (pro forma NOI divided by purchase price plus capital expenditures). We will go over yield on cost in greater detail later, but for now, understand that it is a no-frills metric which is harder to game than IRR. Comparing various deals using the yield on cost metric will provide much greater insight than most other indicators.

The key points about the sponsor, structure, and deal all allow a passive investor to quickly vet investment opportunities coming from sponsors or online syndication groups. Next, let's dive in to learning the full underwriting process, step-by-step.

UNDERWRITING

Beginning to Underwrite/First Steps

Let's begin with the required materials and information needed to fully underwrite a multifamily property:

- The address of the property
- A trailing 12-month financial statement (profit and loss statement).
- A rent roll showing unit type, rent, and additional charges for each unit.
- A trusted underwriting model in Microsoft Excel. Go to www.lscre.com to get your free copy now.
- Optional: Brokers will typically furnish an Offering Memorandum, which assembles a lot of helpful information, including a pro forma and business plan. Projections will often be too simplistic or aggressive to accept at face value,

but are helpful presentations of a strong upside case.

- Optional: Data reports such as Yardi Matrix, CoStar, or Apartment Data Services

More data/research can always be pulled in to inputs and assumptions, but this is often not needed for preliminary underwriting, which will give the clarity to either quickly pass on the deal or submit an LOI at a price that makes sense. For limited partners, preliminary underwriting can allow an efficient decision on whether a proposed investment has merit and/or warrants further research.

The proceeding discussion will refer to the general outline and inputs used in my underwriting model. These are fairly standard inputs across all multifamily models. We will walk through the "Inputs" tab, which is where I spend most of my time, inputting rents, income, expenses, and assumptions, and let the model do the rest. The model calculates important decision metrics like going-in cap rate, stabilized yield on cost, project-level IRR, underwritten debt service coverage ratio, stabilized debt service coverage ratio, and percent of projected returns from cash flow. Let's start at the top of the spreadsheet and work our way through each input.

Property Information
Purchase Price
Pricing Guidance
Physical Vacancy
Year Built

Address

First, we have the basic Property Information section. Here we input the "strike" price (the price expectation from the broker) for Purchase Price and Pricing Guidance. The Purchase Price input is used to make the calculations in the model while the Pricing Guidance input is there just to remind us what the "strike" price is to see how our pricing compares to the guidance after we have changed the purchase price a few times to find the price that allows us to hit our target returns.

Again, to be clear, no calculations in the model use "Pricing Guidance" – it is there strictly for reference. Of course, this is simply the current state of my model – you could choose to build on my model with a feature that displays the underwritten returns at the pricing guidance versus our inputted, target purchase price (hmm…not a bad idea! Don't be surprised if you see an updated model with this feature sometime soon).

Next, Physical Vacancy. This can be found on the rent roll (the more recent the better). For this input, we are looking for the total occupied figure on the rent roll. We are simply looking for a physical occupancy number here, not economic vacancy. Economic vacancy calculates vacancy as a percentage of lost income rather than a percentage of physically occupied units irrespective of the rents for each unit. This input also isn't used for any return calculations, but provides context to the property's current performance and can affect an input we will address later: Going In Vacancy Rate.

Lastly, we have a few more reference inputs that aren't used for calculations: Year Built and Address. The year built, or vintage, of a property, can tell us a lot and helps determine the class of property. The address of a property is of course extremely important as real estate is well known for being all about location, location, location. We'll use the property address later to look up vital information about the property's location such as rental comparables, crime, median household income, and race demographics.

Market Metrics				
	3-Mile*	1-Mile*	Tract**	Block**
Income				
5-Year Pop Growth				
Race				

The next table in the model is Market Metrics. Since we have access to a few of the major apartment data providers, we use CoStar to find the Median Household Income in a 3-mile and 1-mile radius from the property and input those numbers here in this table. We also use CoStar for the 3-mile and 1-mile radiuses for the 5-year projected population growth and race demographics. We use www.justicemap.org to find the Census Tract and Block Median Household Incomes as well as race information (Justice Map does not have population growth projections).

It is important to begin to keep track of all of these income and demographic information for every deal so you can begin to see trends and learn what it means, in number terms, for your property to be located in a good area for your market. In some markets, $40,000 incomes are great, while in others they would point to a no-go zone. Especially for value-add investments, it is important to see the progress of the neighborhood and that incomes support higher rents and a repositioning of the tenant profile if necessary. As above, the Market Metrics table is also for reference only and is not source for any formulas. Nevertheless, this information is extremely important and should inform decisions on other assumptions like pro forma rents, rent growth, and exit cap rate.

Another important metric to look into is crime. To start, google the name and/or address of the property with the word "crime" or "shooting", or try searching the property name/address in Google News. Additionally, you can review crime related information about the property's location on www.city-data.com, www.spotcrime.com, www.crimereports.com, and www.areavibes.com.

Unit Mix & Operating Income

The next section we will focus on is the Unit Mix. Some underwriting models will deviate from this method of inputting the unit mix and will opt instead to input the full rent roll. I am way too lazy to painstakingly input 200 or 400 units into my model, let alone build all of the formulas related to that large of an input requirement. However, it is valuable to be able to quickly read and analyze a rent roll. To do this, it is helpful to have a rent roll in Microsoft Excel format so you can sort and filter the units based on the certain columns such as market rents, lease rents, move-in date, and lease expiration. By sorting units, you can determine the highest rent for each unit type on the property as well as for various interior conditions, such as classic versus renovated units.

Below, I've shown an example inputted unit mix of a 100-unit property which has all one-bedroom/one-bathroom units. The Market column can also be interpreted as current rents or actual rents as they should be reflective of the rent level currently being achieved on the property (less any modest loss to lease). Loss to lease refers to any difference between market rents and lease rents in a property's rent roll. Loss to lease can be attributed to cyclicality in the leasing season or old leases which have yet to renew and capitalize on the market rent growth that has occurred. Investors must be cognizant of the validity of market rents since those can be set by the current owner/manager of the property to any level they desire and simply offset it by loss to lease.

Unit Mix				
Type	# of Units	Market	Pro Forma	SQ FT
1x1	100	$750	$850	650

Rarely should you accept market rents at face value. There are plenty of times when I've underwritten a deal and threw out the market rents from the rent roll and set my own market rents for the property because the loss to lease was so large. I'd rather more accurately reflect lease rents in my market rents than underwrite a large in-place loss to lease. Psychologically, investors have an easier time assuming loss to lease will be "burned off" to a previously anchored level, than they do projecting increases in market rents, even when the revenue increase is the same – I don't want to trick my psychology! The formulas driving the income side of my underwriting model treat increases in rent and reduction in loss to lease equally so it doesn't affect the numbers but it can be confusing initially to see "flat" proforma rents yet a substantial revenue increase due to a reduction in loss to lease.

The Pro Forma column refers to pro forma rents or projected rents in the future. The difference between Market and Pro Forma can often be attributed to the proposed business plan of the investment, whether that be interior renovations, exterior renovations, improved management, or some other strategy. These pro forma rents (in this case it is $850) are used to calculate stabilized Gross Potential Rent. Gross Potential Rent is the total possible rents that would be collected if all units are occupied with no loss to lease or delinquency. If that were true in our example, the property should collect 100 x $850 x 12 = $1,020,000 in gross revenue per year. "Should" is the operative word in that sentence, since that *never* happens and your model should appropriately consider income loss line items such as loss to lease, vacancy, non-revenue units, concessions, employee discounts, and write-offs. Pro forma rents are a very sensitive input, meaning they have a major impact on the results of your underwriting, especially for a value-add investment. A value-add deal can go from great to terrible just by changing pro forma rents by $50.

Another important consideration we will address later is the time required to achieve pro forma. Of course, market rents don't magically turn into pro forma rents the day you buy the property and it often won't happen within the first year of ownership. We will discuss this further in the Stabilization Period section coming up.

The next section is the Operating Income table. Here you will see we have Trailing 12 and Stabilized columns. Since we value the property based on future income, we will focus on stabilized assumptions rather than basing our inputs or decisions on historical figures. That said, it is helpful to see how the property is currently performing and take that into account in our projected stabilization levels.

			Operating Income	
Revenue	Trailing 12	%	Stabilized	%
Gross Potential Rent	$900,000		$1,020,000	13.3%
RUBS				#DIV/0!
Other Income				#DIV/0!
Loss to Lease		0.0%	-$20,400	-2.0%
Vacancy Loss		0.0%	-$71,400	-7.0%
Concessions/Non-Rev		0.00%	-$20,400	-2.00%
Bad Debt		0.00%	-$20,400	-2.00%
EFFECTIVE GROSS INCOM	**$900,000**	**0.0%**	**$887,400**	**-13.0%**

The first column is for Trailing 12-month revenue inputs, obtained from a trailing 12-month profit and loss statement ("T12"). In general, 12 months of information is a good starting point. A year is enough time to smooth out minor irregularities/noise in month-by-month financials. If there is a clear trend in recent months, annualized T3 can be used (= 4 * Final 3 months of T12) for revenue only (for expenses, use T12 – expenses vary seasonally, are not always billed monthly, and are less consistent overall versus income). If using T12, use T12 for all revenue items; if using T3, use T3 for all revenue items.

- **Gross Potential Rent** – This is highlighted in gray in our sheet since it is not input but is calculated from the Unit Mix input in the previous step. In this case, we have $750 rents across 100 one-bedroom units, resulting in $900,000 of GPR. The property's T12 is likely to also have a GPR and it may or may not match up with the calculation in the model. We will use Loss to Lease to adjust for any differences. By calculating the GPR based on the current rents from the unit mix, we are incorporating the most up-to-date rents.

- **RUBS (ratio utility billing system)** – Any income related to utility billback such as water, sewer, electric, and trash. Compare T12 RUBS with total utilities expense to see if there is an opportunity to increase RUBS.

- **Other Income** – This is a catch-all line item for all income other than rents and RUBS such as application fees, late fees, reserved parking, etc. Keep an eye out for irregularities or large one-time payments that may need to be excluded to more accurately reflect recurring Other Income.

- **Loss to Lease** – As previously discussed, loss to lease represents the difference between market rents and lease rents. This is often found on the property's T12 but is only accurate/relevant if the T12's Gross Potential Rent is equal to the one that was generated by your inputted Unit Mix from before. Adjust T12 Loss to Lease input to reflect the Net Potential Rent (Gross Potential Rent minus Loss to Lease) in the T12, i.e. Model Loss To Lease equals T12 Net Potential Rent minus Model GPR.

- **Vacancy Rate** – Revenue lost from vacant units. If a property's T12 has a story it can be better to use T3 vacancy to more accurately reflect current performance.

- **Concessions/Non-Rev** – This line item is for any discounts, concessions, and non-revenue generating units such as units used for storage or down units (units in inoperable condition).

- **Bad Debt** – This line item is for uncollectable rent also known as write-offs. T12s often have a delinquent rent line item and a recovered delinquent rent. If this is the case, be sure to sum both into a net bad debt number. For whatever reason, recovered rent sometimes shows up separately under Other Income.

If the T12 for the property you are underwriting does not have a Gross Potential Rent line item, Loss to Lease, or even Vacancy Rate, and instead just shows a total collected rent number, then it's possible to estimate Gross Potential Rent using the Rent Roll. The Rent Roll should show market rents and lease rents; multiply the difference by 12 to annualize Loss to Lease in the Rent Roll. Vacancy Rate can also be estimated based on the Rent Roll's Physical Vacancy.

With historic financials entered on the T12 side, we can move on to the Stabilized side. This is where some of the real work begins. Similar to the T12 side, Stabilized Gross Potential Rent is also calculated from the previously entered Unit Mix. To begin, I will often simply copy over the T12 RUBS and Other Income inputs to the Stabilized column unless the proposed business plan gives a clear rationale for a higher or lower value. We can pursue more in-depth analysis later to zero in on a more accurate pro forma RUBS and Other Income. The remaining income loss

items are based on percentages of Gross Potential
Rent. I've organized these percentage inputs on the
right-hand side of the "Inputs" tab in the model under
the Assumptions table. We will go over these inputs in
greater detail when we go through those assumptions.

Operating Expenses

The next section is all about operating expenses,
which are fairly sensitive inputs, since they directly
affect the stabilized NOI (net operating income)
calculation, which drives your sale price calculation.
Recall that NOI/price = cap rate; thus NOI/cap rate
= price. This means that once you've calculated
stabilized NOI, you can divide it by a reversion,
terminal or simply "exit" cap rate to derive a projected
sales price. Obviously, our underwriting model is not
quite that simplistic but that is the basic concept
behind income property valuation.

					Operating Expenses
Operating Expenses	Trailing 12	Per Unit	Stabilized	Per Unit	
Payroll		$0		$0	
Contract Services		$0		$0	
Repairs & Maintenance		$0		$0	
Turnover		$0		$0	
Utilities		$0		$0	
Administrative		$0		$0	
Marketing		$0		$0	
Other		$0		$0	
Insurance		$0		$0	
Management Fee	$27,000	$270	$26,622	$266	
Property Taxes	$140,250	$1,403	$140,250	$1,403	
Replacement Reserves	$30,000	$300	$30,000	$300	
Franchise Taxes	$2,979	$30	$2,937	$29	
TOTAL	$200,229	$2,002	$199,809	$1,998	
% of EGI	22.2%		22.5%		
NOI	$699,771	UW	$687,591		

Filling in T12 Expenses is very similar to filling in

T12 Operating Income. You'll need to go through the list of operating expenses and locate or add up the total for each line item.

- **Payroll** – Payroll is any expense related to on-site staff, including health insurance, worker's compensation, temporary staffing and bonuses, but should not include a 3rd party property management fee.

- **Contract Services** – Work done at the property that is not done in-house (this excludes contracted work related to "make readies") such as landscaping, snow removal, and pest control.

- **Repairs & Maintenance** – Things break and tenants complain – best to be proactive and have a good preventative maintenance program, and respond to work orders as quickly as possible. Expenses cost money, of course, but doing this right pays off in tenant satisfaction and retention.

- **Turnover** – Also known as Make Ready, Turnover refers to the cost of preparing vacant units for new tenants. This can include carpet cleaning or replacement, paint, new appliances, and other unit repairs.

- **Utilities** – What the "house" pays varies by

property, but look for electric, water, sewer, trash, and cable. Pay attention to the water bill and the common area electric bill as these numbers can present opportunities for cost savings on older/unrenovated properties.

- **Administrative** – Office-related expenses needed to run the property such as the cost of background checks, printer paper, property management software like ResMan, and phones.

- **Marketing** – Sometimes found in Administrative, Marketing includes listing on Apartments.com, resident retention events such as a pizza renewal party, brochures, and resident referral fees.

- **Other** – This can be for HOA dues or other deal specific costs that are best broken out from other expense groups.

- **Insurance** – Property insurance, general liability, and umbrella insurance. Some properties or lenders may require additional insurance such as flood insurance.

- **Management Fee** – This line item refers to a 3rd party property management fee. Some properties are "self-managed", meaning the owner of the property manages the property him or herself in lieu of hiring a management company. As you can see in our above example of the Operating Expense table of inputs, the T12 Management Fee is already calculated based on market rate (3% of Effective Gross Income in our example). This a more accurate understanding of the property's current expense load. Just because an owner can get by without showing a property management fee on their own P&L doesn't mean that we (the market) should expect such low expenses and thus be willing to pay an inflated value based on cashflow that we would likely not get.

- **Property Taxes** – As with management fee, T12 and Stabilized Property Tax columns are both pre-calculated using the projected forward number. Current tax can be recorded in the Notes area to the right. Since property taxes are usually reassessed on sale, using existing property taxes would overestimate achievable cashflow when calculating the "going in" cap rate. As a buyer, it doesn't help us to know what the seller *was* paying for property taxes (except as a data point in determining pro forma assessed value). Property taxes vary and have a major impact on terminal value – consult a local property tax expert for the best guidance.

- **Replacement Reserves** – These are lender-escrowed reserves usually between $200 to $450/unit/year, intended to be drawn down for recurring capital expenditures such as appliance or flooring replacements. Our model has T12 and Stabilized Replacement Reserves set at $300/unit/year, which is what we typically use for preliminary underwriting. Again, we are less concerned with what the current owner is reserving per the terms of his or her loan agreement. What matters is what *we* will actually see – current (T12) income level adjusted by *our* anticipated replacement reserves. It is also worth noting that Replacement Reserves are here in Operating Expenses to begin with. You sometimes won't see Replacement Reserves "above the line", meaning included in the NOI calculation on profit and loss statements. However, for underwriting purposes, the proper method is to include Replacement Reserves in calculated NOI rather than pushing it "below the line" in the cash flow statement, or as a capital item after NOI is calculated. Keeping Reserves above the line reduces NOI and thus conservatively dampens asset valuation. Furthermore, lenders calculate NOI this way as well, so keeping consistent with their process helps when looking at underwriting to determine appropriate loan assumptions.

- **Franchise Taxes** – Franchise Taxes are not

found everywhere, but they are a reality for Texas multifamily with revenue greater than $1,110,000. Since most of the properties we underwrite are in Texas, Franchise Tax is standard in our underwriting, but it should of course be removed or adjusted when underwriting properties in other states.

As you can see, there is some art to even just copy and pasting T12 numbers over to the underwriting model. Things may need to be rearranged, deleted or made note of. For both T12 operating income and operating expenses, you may need to adjust or reclassify the way that some items are accounted for. For example, sometimes we see a master cable and internet bill paid by the property under Administrative costs in the T12. We prefer to reclassify this expense to Utilities (i.e. reduce Administrative and increase Utilities by that amount) and so will move the cost on both the Trailing 12 and the Stabilized inputs. Use your judgement, which will develop with experience. Consistency is most important – always keeping the same line items in the same categories across different properties you underwrite, to allow like-for-like comparison. The "Underwriting Notes" section towards the end of Broker OMs are also a helpful spot to see where particular items go in typical industry practice, though the specific values projected in Broker OMs may be on the sunny side. Having covered all line items on both the income and expense side, we can now move on to operating assumptions.

Assumptions

*"Never ASSUME, because when you ASSUME, you
make an ASS out of U and ME." –Jerry Belson*

Getting income or expenses wrong can definitely have a dramatic effect on your projected returns, but they can also be easier to get right, especially when working from historical numbers. However, operating assumptions like rent growth and exit cap rate are very sensitive inputs and can dangerously influence the returns. Let's proceed through the various other inputs and assumptions besides income and expenses. Here is the first section of our Assumptions table:

Assumptions		
Acquisition Assumptions		Notes
Acquisition Fee	2.00%	
Transfer Tax	0.00%	
Closing Costs	3.0%	
Cash Reserves	$176,065	
Interest Reserve	$0	

- **Acquisition Fee** – This is a standard closing cost paid by the deal to the sponsor or general partner putting together the investment. In our model, the percentage is based on the purchase price but in practice, the fee can be based on total capitalization, purchase price, total equity, a flat fee, or nonexistent.

- **Transfer Tax** – Some states or counties have a transfer tax that is paid by the buyer, seller or both. This is based on the purchase price.

- **Closing Costs** – Closings costs are costs associated with purchasing property such as third-party reports (environmental report, property condition report, and appraisal), inspections, title fees, and legal fees. We typically use 3% of the purchase price as a preliminary approximation of closing costs. For the modeling purposes, we include property tax and insurance escrows as closing costs even though they are technically reserves and are refunded upon refinance or sale. Lenders typically require the full year's insurance premium to be paid at closing and also require a certain percentage of the anticipated property tax bill to be escrowed based on an escrow analysis. We choose to treat these escrows as costs to keep things simple while also being more conservative.

- **Cash Reserves** – Also called operating capital, this is capital put into the property's operating account or owner account and used to run the business but should also represent some cushion of reserves. There are always unanticipated costs associated with purchase and property takeover and the first few months may be more difficult than anticipated. Having ample reserves that can be depleted and then replenished over the first few months is a wise protocol. As a general rule, we reserve two to three months' worth of operating expenses (here in the screenshot we have two months of operating expenses).

- **Interest Reserve** – For properties that have very little to negative going-in cash flow, the lender will hold back a reserve to make debt service payments. When we underwrite to negative year one cash flows, we will usually input an interest reserve that is 150% to 200% of the negative cash flows. Then we will input an interest reserve draw in the Pro Forma to offset the negative cash flows.

Financing

"Give me a place to stand, a lever long enough and a fulcrum. and I can move the Earth" –Archimedes

Many books have been written on commercial real estate finance so I don't want to spend too much time on financing. Let's briefly, however, go over how to model various financing scenarios in our model.

Senior Debt	
Assumption?	No
Loan to Cost?	Yes
LTC or LTV	75.0%
Duration (Months)	120
Interest Rate	4.25%
Amortization	30
IO Period (Years)	1
Financing Fees	1.50%

- **Assumption?** – A loan assumption is the process of purchasing a property subject to the existing loan on the property. This input should be left as "No" unless you want to model an assumption. To model an assumption, find current loan details, including outstanding loan balance, interest rate, amortization, start date, maturity date, interest-only period, and fees associated with assuming the loan. Instead of "No", input the current loan balance for the loan.

- **Loan to Cost?** – Loans are often measured on

a loan-to-value basis, usually meaning loan amount divided by purchase price. However, many lenders allow an increase of the loan amount by measuring their LTV based on eligible costs including the purchase price plus capital expenditures and even closing costs. You can change this input from "Yes" to "No" to toggle whether you want the loan's proceeds to be based on loan-to-cost or loan-to-value (just purchase price).

- **LTC or LTV** – This is the where you specify how much leverage the loan will be (typically between 70 and 80%).

- **Duration** – This input should only be changed if you're looking to model a refinance in your underwriting. However, incorporating a refinance in your underwriting is not good practice – do this only if absolutely necessary. To model a refi after 36 months of ownership, for example, you would change the Duration to 36 months so the new loan starts on month 37.

- **Interest Rate** – Self-explanatory. However, if you are using floating rate debt, choose "LIBOR Plus" rather than a fixed interest rate. In the cash flow "Pro Forma" tab there is a LIBOR forward curve which can be updated or changed to SOFR (or whatever becomes the prevailing short-term interest rate benchmark index). This will allow you to project floating rate debt as well as stress test interest rates if you would like to input a +1 standard deviation LIBOR or SOFR forward curve.

Senior Debt	
Assumption?	No
Loan to Cost?	Yes
LTC or LTV	75.0%
Duration (Months)	120
Interest Rate	4.25%
Interest Rate	30
LIBOR Plus	1
Financing Fees	1.50%

- **Amortization** – Amortization is the process of paying down debt through regular principal payments made with the monthly mortgage payment. Permanent financing for commercial real estate and multifamily typically amortizes on a 30-year schedule, meaning the debt would be fully paid off if principal and interest payments were made over the course of 30 years. This rarely happens as most permanent financing has a 10-year term, leaving due a balloon payment of the remaining loan balance after 10 years. Bridge loans typically include no amortization and have interest-only payments for the full term of the loan, which is typically two to three years.

- **IO Period** – Loans often have an interest-only period for the first one to five years of the loan. As mentioned before, bridge loans are interest-only for the entire term of the loan. This input allows you to specify how many years the loan is interest-only for. In our example, only interest is paid on the loan for the first year and the payments in the subsequent nine years include principal and interest payments.

- **Financing Fees** – Loans often include an upfront fee paid at closing, called a financing fee. Additional fees here include a mortgage broker fee. Lenders typically charge a 0.5% to 1% financing fee and mortgage brokers charge between 0.5% to 1%.

Stabilization Assumptions

The stabilization period or process is the most difficult and unique part of the construction of a value-add underwriting model. Models vary in how they project operations and financials throughout stabilization and/or renovation.

Our model works like this. The Gross Potential Rent, RUBS, Other Income, Loss to Lease, Concessions/Non-Rev, and Bad Debt line items on the Operating Income side all start in month one at the T12 level. Next, we use a Stabilization Months assumption which forecasts how long it will to take to bring these income items from the current in-place figures to the pro forma or stabilized assumptions. The change occurs linearly or in uniform fashion over the months of the Stabilization Period.

For example, a $100 rent increase over 10 months, would be calculated as a $10 rent increase per month for 10 months. In our example below, if a property has 200 units with market rents of $800 and pro forma rents of $900, we project 24 months to renovate all 200 units to achieve $900 market rents across the board. Notice that Vacancy Loss here differs from the T12 figure – we use a separate Going In Vacancy Rate input that lets us adjust the starting vacancy rate. There is often a spike in vacancy at takeover due to the likely NTVs, evictions, and skips that we will be dealing with as we start working to improve the property. Some other metrics such as Bad Debt could also increase for the first few months of stabilization. However, for simplicity, we assume Bad Debt begins at the T12 level and trends towards the stabilized Bad Debt assumption over the course of the Stabilization Period. Slightly overstating Going-in Vacancy can help account for some of these other potential losses early on in the investment.

I believe this is the simplest yet most accurate way to model a value-add business plan. Models sometimes get very complex with calculations that track the number of units being renovated per month and the rent premium pre- and post-renovation. A much simpler way to go about this is to consider the time realistically needed to renovate the number of units required while at the same time maintaining a certain occupancy level or trend. For example, if Going-In Vacancy is 50%, then units renovated per month can be more aggressive, and thus Stabilization Months input can be lower. Conversely, if the plan is to maintain 95% occupancy while programmatically renovating all 200 units, that will take a lot longer. One of the biggest mistakes that people make is to be overly aggressive on expected stabilization timeline. We all know that projects, especially in construction, take longer than anticipated, and there are always unforeseen bumps in the road. Best to be conservative and err on the side of a longer stabilization period.

Another significant detail in the model is whether to begin the annual rent escalator during or after the stabilization period. In our model, we wait until the pro forma rents and assumptions are achieved before rents start escalating at the annual rent growth assumption (usually 2% to match inflation). Many models run the annual rent growth throughout the entire duration of the model, starting from month one. This will of course make the deal look better than the other method. Neither way is necessarily correct, but be aware which method your model uses. Let's proceed to the Stabilization Assumptions section in the model.

Stabilization Assumptions	
Stabilization Months	24
Interior Cost Per Door	$5,000
# of Units to Rehab	200
Exterior Budget	$400,000
Going In Vacancy Rate	8.0%

- **Stabilization Months** (discussed at length above) – months needed to achieve our stabilized assumptions (pro forma rents, stabilized vacancy rate, etc.).

- **Interior Cost Per Door** – Assuming you have budgeted interior renovations or repairs, you can input the average cost per unit for these capital expenditures. This number is multiplied by the number below it (# of Units to Rehab) to calculate the total interior budget. In the example above, we assume a fairly typical renovation for B/C class apartments in Texas of $5,000/unit for all 200 units.

- **# of Units to Rehab** – Input the number of units to be renovated as part of capital expenditures ("capex").

- **Exterior Budget** – Here we assume $400,000
  or $2,000/unit for exterior renovations. This
  could include roofing, siding, pavement,
  plumbing, exterior lighting, fencing, and
  adding/improving amenities to the property.

- **Going-in Vacancy Rate** – As previously
  discussed, this input represents projected
  month one vacancy rate which will then
  escalate linearly up to the Stabilized Vacancy
  Rate over months of the Stabilization Period.

Having covered the process of stabilization and
capex assumptions, we now reach the Stabilized
Assumptions that we expect to achieve by the end of
the stabilization period, and that are used for stabilized
NOI calculation. These inputs relate mostly to the
Stabilized Operating Income line items that we
previously passed over since they are percentage
driven. While our rent doesn't start growing year-over-
year until the property stabilizes, Operating Expenses
grow starting at purchase since we can't put inflation
on hold.

Stabilized Assumptions	
Asset Management Fee	2.0%
Property Management Fee	3.0%
Property Tax Rate	2.75%
Projected Assessed Value	$8,500,000
Annual Rent Increase	2.0%
Annual Expense Increase	2.0%
Property Tax Increase	3.0%
Vacancy Rate	7.0%
Loss to Lease	2.0%
Concessions/Non-Rev	2.00%
Bad Debt	2.00%
Reserves Per Unit	$300

- **Asset Management Fee** – Real estate ventures typically include an AM fee. Usually assessed on Effective Gross Revenue; standard fee is 1% to 2%, depending on the Property Management Fee and size of property.

- **Property Management Fee** – We previously discussed the 3rd party property management fee in the Operating Expenses section. We input that fee here to account for the ongoing cost of management throughout the life of the underwriting. This fee is also assessed on Effective Gross Income.

- **Property Tax Rate** – Also known as millage rate, the property tax rate can be found on the county assessor's website.

- **Projected Assessed Value** – The assessed

value for property tax purposes can often vary substantially from the purchase price. This is why it is very important to consult a property tax advisor. In our example deal here, we have a purchase price of $10,000,000 and are assuming an 85% assessment ratio (assessed value divided by purchase price), resulting in an assessed value of $8,500,000.

- **Annual Rent Increase** – This is a rent escalator which factors rent growth into the underwriting model. Rent growth can be contentious since it is widely known to be a lever that sponsors pull to boost their returns, and a very sensitive lever at that. Rent growth is a sensitive input because it is a compounding assumption. The rate at which you set rent growth will compound every year throughout the model. Therefore, longer hold periods are even more sensitive to this input. We rarely project rent growth above 2% because we want the numbers to support the returns of the investment without future rent increases. Rather than "bank" on future rent increases, we can accept a lower underwritten return for an investment we think is particularly safe or strong and is poised to outperform due to future growth.

- **Annual Expense Increase** – The annual expense escalator should track inflation (typically 2 to 3%). Unlike rent increases, which begins after stabilization – once renovations are complete and proforma rents are achieved – this grows from day 1. In our model all expenses grow at this assumed rate except Property Management Fee, Property Taxes, Reserves, and Franchise Taxes. Property Management Fee is based on Effective Gross Income so it will increase by the percentage of EGI increase. Property Tax increases are projected separately since property taxes can increase significantly in certain circumstances. Reserves typically stay the same throughout an investment, such as $300 per unit per year. Similar to Property Management Fee, Franchise Taxes are based on revenue and therefore escalate at the same rate of revenue increases.

- **Property Tax Increase** – As mentioned above, property tax growth can vary based on the location of the property and your business plan. Therefore, it is nice to have an input to increase the property taxes at a different rate than the rest of the operating expenses. For example, in Houston and other Texas markets, the appraiser is income driven and will adjust the assessed value according to the property's performance from an income perspective by using an implied cap rate calculation. Thus, if the plan is to buy a property, renovate it, and raise rents by 20%, expect similar increase in property taxes. This is often omitted from investors' calculus.

- **Vacancy Rate** – The minimum vacancy rate

that agency lenders are allowed to underwrite to is 5%, so we do the same. However, most of the time our projected stabilized Vacancy Rate is 7% to 10%. We get this stabilized Vacancy Rate from market data that tells us of the vacancy rates for comparable properties nearby.

- **Loss to Lease** – Loss to Lease refers to the difference between a property's market rents and the average actual rents. We use 2% as our standard Loss to Lease; sometimes this will be 0%, if the property currently has a gain to lease (in-place rents that are higher than market rents).

- **Concessions/Non-Rev** – This line item is very market and property dependent. Different areas have different levels of concessions and you may choose to provide discounted or free apartments to some of your on-site employees (employee discounts and free units belong in this line item).

- **Bad Debt** – This refers to uncollectable rent, also called write offs. Nicer properties with a better tenant demographic tend to have lower Bad Debt. We typically underwrite Bad Debt within a range of .5% to 2.5%.

- **Reserves Per Unit** – Here we input the

lender-mandated replacement reserves which are usually around $300 per unit per year for the type of property we buy (class B and C multifamily).

We have covered Unit Mix, Operating Income, Operating Expenses, as well as the stabilization/stabilized assumptions. All that remains in this preliminary cash flow and sale analysis is projecting the sale.

Exit Assumptions

"Real estate is an imperishable asset, ever increasing in value. It is the most solid security that human ingenuity has devised. It is the basis of all security and about the only indestructible security." –Russell Sage

Exit assumptions are inputs related to the sale of the property. Here we are inputting a Terminal Cap Rate and a hold period to determine the projected sale price. As with purchase, there are sale costs including legal and title fees, sales broker commission, and financing fees or prepayment penalties for early loan payoff. Below is the Exit Assumptions table from our underwriting model.

Exit Assumptions	
Terminal Cap Rate	6.00%
Commission/Title/Legal	1.5%
Hold Time (Years)	5
Transfer Tax	0.00%
Financing Fees	1.0%

- **Terminal Cap Rate** – Also known as exit or

reversion cap rate. Projected T12 NOI at Sale divided by Cap Rate equals Projected Sale Price. Much has been said about exit cap rates and for good reason; this is perhaps the most sensitive input in the model. Even a small change in the exit cap rate changes the projected sale price significantly, which drives a significant portion of the total returns, especially for value-add investments where most of the value comes from appreciation rather than cashflow. In our example deal, the projected 5-year sale price is $13,869,379 at a 6% Terminal Cap Rate. However, at a 6.5% exit cap rate, the projected sale price is $12,802,504. This change in exit cap rate (leading to an 8.3% increase in projected sale price) changes the project-level IRR for our hypothetical deal from 17.3% to 13.4% – a major difference! Since most real estate investments use leverage, changes in projected sale price are multiplied. We will discuss exit cap rates in further depth in the Exit Assumptions section and learn how they and sales prices can be determined and sometimes manipulated.

- **Commission/Title/Legal** – These are estimated closing costs – sales commissions, title fees, and legal fees to be paid upon closing of the sale. We use a percentage of the projected sales price for this approximation, which is usually 1% to 3% based on the type and size of properties we buy and sell.

- **Hold Time** – Our model accepts a hold period anywhere from three to ten years, and the cash flows and future sale scenario will adjust accordingly. For heavier value-add deals requiring a bridge loan, we underwrite to a three-year exit, rather than assuming a longer hold period and a refinance. For deals bought with permanent financing, we typically underwrite to a five-year hold. Although true hold time may vary from our underwriting depending on the business plan, underwriting consistent hold periods across similar deals (3-year fix and flips; 5-year stabilized holds) allows us to best compare the projected returns of various deals.

- **Transfer Tax** – Some states have a real estate transfer tax which can be modeled here. Alternatively, if you have a different closing cost you wish to incorporate, you simply rename the Transfer Tax line item and input the desired percentage of projected sales price for the cost. For example, this could be used for a Disposition Fee, which some sponsors charge as a percentage of sale price.

- **Financing Fees** – Here you can input a fee paid to the lender to pay off the existing loan. This could be an exit fee, which is typically 1% on bridge loans, or yield maintenance, or defeasance. However, I have never seen yield maintenance or defeasance modeled into an underwriting, despite so many deals being financed with long-term fixed rate debt bearing yield maintenance or defeasance prepayment penalties today. Yield maintenance can be extremely costly, which could force a sale "on assumption", i.e., subject to the buyer assuming the in-place financing, avoiding an exit/prepayment penalty for the seller. If the plan is to sell on assumption, it is prudent to account for this via a slightly higher exit cap rate to reflect the likely less favorable sale conditions of assuming an above-market interest rate loan or a loan with no interest-only payments component. In any case, in my opinion, it is prudent and appropriate to include some financing fee in your underwriting to be conservative, unless you have specifically planned to either hold until the prepayment penalty ends, or to sell on assumption.

And there you have it! That's the "Inputs" tab in our multifamily acquisition underwriting model. By now, you should be able to put together a preliminary underwriting model and begin to evaluate important metrics such as going in cap rate ("Adjusted Trailing Cap Rate" in the model), stabilized yield on cost ("Return on Cost" in the model), project level IRR, and cash on cash yield. But before we go there, we need to first perform rental and sales comparables analyses in order to support the viability and appropriateness of our purchase price, projected sales price, and pro forma rent and occupancy assumptions.

RENTAL & SALES COMPARABLES

Rental Comparables

Performing a rental comparables analysis, or rent comps, is the most time-consuming aspect of underwriting a multifamily investment. If a business plan leaves rents unchanged rent comps may be less important. However, the bulk of deals we look at have a value-add component where we renovate the property and improve management to capture higher market rents. When underwriting increased rents, rent comps are needed to justify the increases based on the market. Beyond rent increases, rent comps also support a lease-up business plan, or a situation where the subject property's vacancy rate is higher than the market vacancy rate by showing that strong occupancy is possible at target rents – of course the lower the rents, relative to the market, the easier it will be to fill the property; the higher the rents, the tougher it will be.

The best rent comps are properties of a similar vintage and condition (to your subject property's post-renovated condition) near the subject property. Proximity of a comparable property is paramount since neighborhoods can change block-to-block in quality and rent levels. A reasonable distance for comps is anywhere from one to three miles, depending on the density of the area and the variation of demographics.

We check the area demographics of the subject property and compare it to a comp's location information. For example, we may have found a comparable property only two miles away with $150 higher rents, but if that area has higher median incomes and a more desirable demographic mix, our "comparable" may not be so comparable. Similarly, a property next door could have higher rents, but also be a newer property with nine-foot ceilings, instead of our eight-foot ceilings. An older property with eight-foot ceilings will always struggle to compete with a nine-foot ceiling property.

Another factor to consider are additional rent charges, including utility billbacks, or ratio utility billing systems (RUBS). Some apartment complexes add additional monthly charges into the cost of the apartment; others include all costs in the rent amount. For example, if a unit includes a washer/dryer, there may be an additional charge for the washer/dryer along with the base rent, such as a $50 monthly fee. Other complexes may choose to just factor the increased value of the washer/dryer into higher rents. Take this into account as you compare your subject property to rental comps. For example, a nearby property with $50 higher rents could seem a strong candidate for a $50 rent increase. However, if that property has washers/dryers included in the unit, while our subject property does not, customers will likely rent there rather than accept the rent increase. We could build washer/dryer installation costs in to the business plan for this $50 upside, but it would be a mistake to just simply assume that a $50 rental increase is achievable without providing any additional value to the residents and community.

Another big example, as mentioned above, is RUBS. Most properties bill residents for a portion of the utilities such as water, sewer, and trash. Properties within a given submarket will generally have the same RUBS protocol, making the rent comp analysis a little easier. However, some properties, especially older ones, have no utility billbacks, a.k.a. "all bills paid" (ABP). An ABP community builds all utilities into rent, which simplifies tenants' bill paying experience. Although this sounds simpler, it is not as common these days. We much prefer RUBS, especially with a variable usage formula, because residents feel the impact of the utility usage and generally are more energy/water conscious if they know they are partially paying for it.

To get this granular level of detail on rent comparable properties such as RUBS charges and other charges, you must call the comparable properties directly and "mystery shop" them as if you were a prospective resident. There's no script or a secret formula. I'm just friendly and ask questions as if I really were a prospective resident. This helps add color to our rent comparables and really understand where our target property's rents are versus the market. Rent comp information can also be obtained from Google searches, Apartments.com, and paid apartment data services such as Yardi Matrix, CoStar, and ALN Apartment Data. In summary, rent comparables are essential in order to create and support pro forma rents and stabilized vacancy rate, both of which are sensitive inputs that heavily influence the potential value of the property.

Sales Comparables

Sales comparables are also important to the underwriting process, but more as a sanity check of our potential purchase price as well as our projected future exit price. This mainly affects terminal/exit cap rate input, because exit cap heavily factors in to determining the projected sale valuation.

Look at sales comps to back up both the purchase and sale price of an investment. We want to buy at a reasonable price given quality and location and sell at a reasonable price given quality and location.

For value-add investments, sales comps are particularly important since sale price will be well above purchase price. This increased sale price typically accounts for much of the value in a value-add deal. As buyers, we justify both paying more than the asset might be worth on an ongoing cashflow basis and further investing in capex improvements on the grounds that we can increase cashflow and sell for more after we improve it. In this case, the best justification for higher exit price is the increased NOI that the next buyer will use to value the property – ideally both on the revenue side – better units demand higher rents – and on the expense side, if we can cut costs. In hot markets deals can trade several times in a row with each new buyer paying richly while planning further "value-adds." The success or failure of most value-add business plans depends on being able to sell for substantially more than our cost basis (purchase price plus capex), so it is essential that market sales comps support the projected sales price through previous sales of comparable properties at similar price levels.

At the time of this writing in early 2020, the real estate cycle is in its later stages and prices are at cyclical and all-time highs. Because of this, it is rare to see an investment with a projected sales price in three to five years that is actually supported by recent sales comps. Nonetheless, this remains the goal when looking to sales comps to judge whether our proposed exit is feasible. However, for investments in strong growth markets relying on market rent growth and price appreciation, especially forecasted over a 10-year hold period, finding true sales comps that support this 10-year exit price will likely be impossible and impractical. For a buy-and-hold strategy, sales comps are less useful for proving out the potential exit price than they are for establishing that the purchase price we pay is reasonable. Furthermore, sales comps take a back seat to yield metrics (cap rate, yield on cost, cash on cash) for longer term holds focused on cash flow.

Sales Comps can be simpler than rent comps as far as analysis goes, but getting a hold of the information is not always as easy. Market data for sales can be thin for non-disclosure states such as Texas.

As with rent comps, comparable properties for sales should be as similar to the subject property as possible. The main criteria to focus on for similarities are location/distance, property age, property condition, average rents, and date of sale. Other considerations are the debt used or assumed in the sale and nuances such as a LIHTC (Low Income Housing Tax Credit) and/or LURA (Land Use Restriction Agreement) and other rental rate restrictions.

Sales can be compared using cap rates, price per unit, and price per square foot. All three are important metrics as they each tell a different story and are each more relevant in certain instances. Cap rates are difficult to obtain for sales since net operating income isn't reported uniformly (or honestly), since there are many moving parts like adjustments for property tax increases, or whether NOI includes/excludes replacement reserves. Additionally, many buyers are buying with a value-add business plan which makes the going-in cap rate even less telling about the true value of the property since value-add deals are typically bought at a compressed cap rate due to the future upside. Nevertheless, it is good to get some cap rate data on comparable sales which can be obtained from data services such as CoStar. The best way to get cap rate data is by asking your trusted broker relationships. It is a broker's business to stay on top of all of the trades happening in the market, including who the buyers and sellers are, pricing, and even the terms and conditions. Another good way to gather indirect sales comps is by looking at loans. Apartment data providers usually show loan data from which we can impute a purchase price, though this should be taken with a grain of salt since LTV is uncertain. To impute value from the loan amount, divide the loan amount by your assumed loan-to-value (LTV).

In the multifamily market, most people are focused

on price per unit which is a great way to compare properties' values. However, price per door, similar to cap rate, can also be skewed or at least not tell the full picture. For example, the price per unit of a small complex of 400 square foot studios is not comparable to the price per unit of a townhome development with 1,200 square foot homes. Even if two properties have the same average square footage per unit, a difference in rent (often arising from quality differences) could drive a significant difference in price per unit. Price per square foot accounts for smaller versus larger units but misses key information like number of kitchens (which price per unit does) or bathrooms.

In the end, cap rate, price per unit, and price per square foot all matter, and comparable properties used should be as similar as possible to avoid the mismatches noted above. Since sales comps are typically harder to find than rent comps, a larger radius from the subject property may be needed (up to five miles). Additionally, it is appropriate to include some "reach" comps which may not really be comparable properties but can shed some light as to how high the market goes. For example, a class B property likely cannot be value-added enough to compete with newly constructed class A product, but it still may be helpful to check the prices of class A properties to see what the market ceiling is. This can also be used to support your evaluation of discount to class A or replacement cost.

Understand when and how the sales comp was purchased – of course, yesterday's sale data could point to today's value being more or less, depending on the growth and real estate/credit cycle since the sale. Also important is the debt used in the sale, since debt has a huge impact on values. For example, if the property was a recent sale but subject to an unattractive CMBS loan assumption, which included a low assumed loan balance, above-market interest rate, and less than 30 years of amortization, then the value of the property was significantly hampered in that sale. If that same sale had occurred "free and clear", i.e. without being subject to the existing financing, then the property would have sold for much more (potentially 10% to 20% more). These examples, as well as the points previously discussed, are important to consider when performing sales comps, especially if they are to be used to support or discredit a potential investment.

Now that you can analyze rent and sales comps to support your underwriting assumptions, you are ready to evaluate the outputs of the hard work you have entered into the model.

EVALUATING THE RESULTS

"Do you know the only thing that gives me pleasure? It's to see my dividends coming in." —John D. Rockefeller

Now that you have put together a preliminary underwriting model you now can evaluate the prospective returns of the investment. The universal standard measure of returns on alternative investments across real estate, private equity, and venture capital is the internal rate of return (IRR). The IRR is the discount rate which makes the net present value (NPV) of the stream of cash flows equal to zero. Without spending a lot of time working with, experimenting, and thinking about NPV and IRR, this definition can be difficult to conceptualize. To break it down, the goal of the IRR calculation is to take lumpy, uneven cash flows (large initial outlay, lower to no cash flow initially, then larger cash flows, maybe a refinance, and finally a sale) and smooth them out over the hold period in order to mimic the compounded rate of return achieved in an interest-bearing vehicle such as a high yield savings account. This smoothed out return calculation can then be used to compare returns between various investments with varying return profiles, such as a more stable cash flowing multifamily investment versus a development project, which could have no cash flow for the first two years.

The key to understanding net present value (NPV) and internal rate of return (IRR) is the concept of time value of money, which underpins all investing. Investors invest money today to make more tomorrow. However, because money is useful today for necessities or enjoyment, investors prefer money today over money tomorrow or some other point in the future. Similarly, money today versus money in the future is more valuable from an investment perspective due to inflation and opportunity cost. This is the impetus for the discount rate. The discount rate is the rate at which money in the future, in increments of years, is discounted in order to derive its value in today's terms. For example, using a 10% discount rate, receiving $1,000,000 of cash flow one year from today is worth $909,091 today in net present value terms and receiving $1,000,000 two years from today is worth only $826,446. The reason the numbers are not round such as $900,000 and $810,000 is due to the compounding nature of the discount rate. The goal of investing is to create more money in the future that is more valuable than your opportunity cost discounted back to present value.

Since an IRR is a discount rate, you can evaluate the prospective IRR against your own opportunity cost to create a similar return taking on a similar level of risk. So, if you believe your typical multifamily investment returns a 15% IRR with a normal amount of risk, you would invest in a proposed multifamily investment if the IRR was 15% or greater, assuming the risk level was comparable.

However, even with a strong understanding of internal rate of return and how it relates to typical return profiles for multifamily investments, IRR is still a very subjective metric, sensitive to various inputs and manipulation.

Another common metric is cash on cash – the annual cash flow as a percentage of the total equity invested in the project. Ongoing Cash on Cash yield doesn't consider the future sale of the investment, which can drive the bulk of the returns in an IRR calculation and can be more speculative. Thus, cash on cash is considered more reliable, but is not most often discussed, since it is missing a big piece of the return puzzle (reversion analysis). Cash on cash yield can be calculated in a table for each year of the investment, or averaged across the hold period to give a single number. However, besides ignoring the future sale, cash on cash alone also doesn't distinguish between debt structures, such as between a full-term interest-only loan or amortization. For example, a five-year investment with a projected average cash on cash of 8% might sound great. But it could be less impressive if financed with full interest-only debt, resulting in zero principal paydown during the five-year hold. Conversely, a strong investment could have a lower cash on cash because the loan is fully amortizing on a 30-year schedule or shorter, principal payments taking up free cash flow. This is just one example of why evaluating investment returns cannot be reduced to simply looking at IRR and cash on cash and calling it a day.

Because of the complexity and all of the variables that factor into IRR and cash on cash calculations, some people try to simplify it all down by just discussing return levels via cap rates. A capitalization rate, or cap rate, is the net operating income divided by purchase price. This metric ignores any financing, while cash on cash does not, to create the simplest indication of return level for an investment. Additionally, there are many different cap rates, which can cause confusion when you're trying to speak the same language with another investor (my 5% cap rate may drastically differ from your 5% cap rate). For example, a cap rate can be calculated based on historical financials, such as a trailing 12-month cap rate or future cap rates can be calculated based on year one or later projections. However, these cap rate calculations typically miss closing costs, capital expenditures, and future revenue potential.

The cleanest solution to these issues and the simplest yet most robust return metric is something called return on cost, or yield on cost. Yield on cost is a more telling version of a cap rate since it factors projected income as well as the capital expenditures budgeted to achieve said projected income.

Value-add returns depend on *creating* stabilized cash flows for less than the cost of simply buying the same cash flows already fully realized. For example, with a 6% market cap rate on stabilized cashflows, a value-add business plan would seek to grow the investment's operating cap rate (NOI divided by purchase price plus capital expenditures) to at least 7% (preferably 8%). If successful, you have "built" cash flows for an 8% cap and can sell those cash flows at a 6% cap, realizing substantial capital appreciation.

However, in today's competitive market, many operators are buying that same value-add deal at a 4– 4.5% cap rate and only raising their operating cap to 6– 6.5%. This means the buyer could put in serious effort to renovate, raise rents, and lower vacancy – taking on substantial risk – and still not achieve much increase in equity or current yield. Worse still, the buyer sustained low cash flows during the stabilization period to achieve the only-slightly-higher stabilized yield on cost. Truthfully, this buyer would have been better off buying a core/core-plus asset and clipping a coupon from the start. This mathematical realization is why I urge investors not to be dazzled by business plans that boast $200 rent bumps and eye-catching "before and after" interior renovation pictures. At high enough entry prices, such large rent increases may be needed just to bring return on cost above the cost of debt.

A similar metric to the operating cap rate just discussed is one that I call *unlevered, stabilized, untrended return on cost* (or just return on cost). I often speak with investors who have grown weary of easily-manipulated

IRR projections; return on cost is an elegant metric that cuts out the noise of growth projections, exit cap rates, and financing assumptions. This return on cost metric is calculated using *pro forma* NOI (without growth assumptions), divided by purchase price plus capital expenditures, and is independent of capital structure. This calculation gives the clearest picture of whether or not an investment has true value-add potential. The only thing it misses is the stabilization time factored in to achieve the *pro forma* NOI. Of course, the combination of time to stabilize and execution risk are why investors have historically demanded a higher return on cost for a value-add deal over a core-plus or core investment. I believe a strong risk-adjusted return for a value-add investment is anywhere from 100 to 200 basis points over market cap rates for stabilized, comparable product. However, since we typically use market cap rate plus 50 bps to calculate our exit cap, we are often aiming for 150 to 250 bps over prevailing market cap rates for our return on cost. For the most part, we are currently buying in areas that warrant 6.5% exit cap projections, calling for an 8%+ stabilized return on cost target. Before even looking at project-level IRR, we look at this figure. Next, we consider unlevered IRR (targeting 9–12%), which factors in growth and sales assumptions, but not financing. These are *true* value-add returns and are more than commensurate with the execution risk of the business plan.

Even if a deal fails to meet these hurdles (few do, especially in primary or growth markets), we may still consider the investment if it exhibits *true* positive leverage. A well-priced deal has a higher return on cost than the amortized debt constant (principal and interest payments as a percentage of principal). While quality property can still be bought for cap rates above interest rates, creating nominal positive leverage, trouble can arise if and when amortization begins. Even 30-year amortization has a major impact on total debt service, which is exacerbated in a low-interest rate environment. A loan with a 3% interest rate would turn into a 5.06% debt constant when amortization kicks in! Here are some amortized debt constants for given loan interest rates that show the increasing severity of this reality with lower interest rates.

- 3% interest rate = 5.06% amortized debt constant
- 4% interest rate = 5.73% amortized debt constant
- 5% interest rate = 6.44% amortized debt constant
- 6% interest rate = 7.19% amortized debt constant
- 7% interest rate = 7.98% amortized debt constant

At a 6% interest rate amortization increases debt service by 20%. At 4% interest rates, amortization increases debt service by over 43% – more than doubling the marginal impact. Many investors are banking on rent growth to bail them out of this massive jump in debt service when their interest only period expires. When evaluating the merits of investments, we look for a comfortable spread between our yield and our amortized debt constant, as well as a spread over our projected exit cap rate. While paying down principal via amortization isn't our idea of an optimal investment strategy, it always makes sense to evaluate fully-amortized debt payments to confirm that our anticipated cash flows are sufficient and have the ability to ride out a loan's principal and interest payments, even through a downturn.

Obviously, a lot more was discussed here than just return on cost but understanding the context around the metric, such as the way it relates to the cost of debt as well as its relation to market cap rates, is important. Another benefit of return on cost is that it cannot be manipulated by a high annual rent growth rate, nor can it be manipulated by an unrealistically low exit cap (driving up the projected sales price). Being able to evaluate these nuances of projections such as return on cost, DSCR, operating expense ratio is imperative to truly be able to qualify a strong investment.

Now that you have a better idea how to evaluate a multifamily investment on a deeper level, rather than just accepting the projected IRR and cash on cash at face value, let's explore how sensitivity analyses can further inform our investment decision-making.

SENSITIVITY ANALYSES

"Never forget the 6-foot-tall man who drowned crossing the stream that was 5 feet deep on average." –Howard Marks

Now that you know how to fill out the underwriting model with revenue, expenses, debt structure, and sale value and can justify these inputs with rent and sales comps, you're ready to develop and evaluate sensitivity analyses.

Breakeven Occupancy

The most commonly discussed stress test is the breakeven occupancy metric. Here is the Occupancy Stress table on the Sensitivities tab of our model, based partially on some of the hypothetical inputs we went through earlier in the book.

Occupancy Stress		
	Min DSCR	Breakeven
Month 1	83.4%	78.3%
Year 1	81.2%	76.3%
Year 2	86.4%	80.0%

There is actually quite a bit of information packed into this little table above. First let's define breakeven occupancy as well as what a minimum DSCR is and how that relates to occupancy. Breakeven occupancy is the economic occupancy rate at which there is enough revenue to pay for all operating expenses and debt service (in our model, this includes replacement reserves but does not include asset management fees or any other "below the line" cash flow items). To calculate this percentage, divide total expenses (including debt service) by the total potential rent (I calculate this by taking effective gross income and adding back vacancy). This method has some defects such as not accounting for lower property management fees if revenue falls. Nor does it account for lower Other Income/RUBS or changes in Concessions and Bad Debt as occupancy decreases. Nevertheless, this straightforward breakeven occupancy calculation is pretty robust and gives a strong indication of the investment's ability to cover its current liabilities in a downside scenario.

In the table above, we also have a column for minimum DSCR occupancy, which is the occupancy needed to maintain the minimum debt service coverage (DSCR) ratio (net operating income divided by debt service). Minimum DSCR is one metric used by lenders to determine the maximum leverage offered against a property. Typically, minimum DSCR is 1.25x, meaning that NOI must be 125% of debt service (including principal and interest). However, in our Occupancy Stress table, we calculate the Min DSCR column by current debt service rather than just based on fully amortized debt service. As you can see in the table, the Min DSCR breakeven occupancy when the interest-only period ends after the first year of the loan, increasing the debt service payments substantially, despite higher income from rent increases.

It is important to understand how amortizing debt payments affect an investment's cash flow and risk. On the one hand, interest-only payments require less cashflow for the property to stay current on the mortgage; on the other hand, no principal is paid down, so there is significant balloon risk to the deal. Conversely, amortization increases the debt service load on the property but also reduces the overall outstanding debt, which decreases the overall riskiness of the investment.

Refinance/Exit Test

One of the most important, if not *the* most important, stress tests of a multifamily investment is the refinance/exit test, or just exit test. The reason being, the two biggest risks of actually losing money in a multifamily or any real estate investment are loan default risk and loan maturity risk.

Default risk is the risk of not being able to meet your debt service and ending up in default which may force the lender to foreclose on the property. Maturity risk is the that the loan comes due and the outstanding principal balance cannot be repaid due to unfavorable capital markets environment or poor property performance. This puts the investment in a bind, forcing either a sale at a bad time, or a refinance to lower loan balance, with a capital call for additional equity. In my opinion, maturity risk is an even greater risk than default risk since it is harder to model or account for.

The way to prepare for and stress loan maturity risk is by performing a refinance/exit test. This test involves forecasting the loan's unpaid principal balance at loan maturity as well as the base case net operating income and property valuation at loan maturity. With this information, a hypothetical refinance can be projected to see if a new loan could be large enough to pay off the existing loan upon maturity. Of course, the base case assumptions should pass this refinance test with flying colors. Where this becomes interesting is when you start to stress the net operating income and property valuation upon loan maturity to see if the

existing loan would still be able to be refinanced
without the need for additional equity. Below are the
parameters of our typical exit test.

Refinance Exit Test Assumptions		
	Inputs	Result
Refi in Month	120	PASS
Operational Shock	10%	-24.3%
Capital Markets Shock		
Interest Rate Increase	25%	6.25%
Refi Cap Rate Increase	15%	6.90%

The Inputs column are inputs to change the
parameters of the exit test while the Result column
shows the resulting calculations. First, the term of the
loan should be inputted for "Refi in Month". In this
case, we have a 10-year fixed-rate loan. Next, we can
modify the "Operational Shock", defined as a decrease
in effective gross income, or revenue, as a percentage.
In this case, we reduce revenue by 10%, which to the
right gives a 24.3% decline in NOI (this relationship
varies as different properties have varying expense
loads as a percentage of revenue). Lastly, we have a
"Capital Markets Shock", which would be a change in
market interest rates as well as valuations (cap rate) at
the time of refinance. Using these various shocks to
income as well as how that income is valued results in
some pretty interesting stress test results. Let's examine
the results.

	Current	Base Case
NOI	$897,017	$897,017
Valuation	$14,950,288	$14,950,288
Loan Amount	$7,134,251	$11,212,716
LTV	48.0%	75.0%
DSCR	1.78x	1.56x

The first column, Current, shows our projected T12 NOI and the property's valuation based on the input for refinance cap rate at the time of refinance (120 months or at the end of our 10-year model). The Current column also shows the existing loan's remaining balance ($7,134,251), which is 48% LTV based on our $14,950,288 valuation. Lastly, the current debt service coverage ratio (DSCR) is 1.78x, calculated by dividing current NOI by current debt service. We include DSCR in this table because lenders will underwrite the projected new loan to a DSCR of 1.25x. In times of market turmoil, lenders tighten up their criteria, so 1.30x DSCR may even be a better assumption to work with.

The Base Case column uses the same information as Current (based on the assumptions already input in the model) to calculate a refinance into a new loan of $11,212,716, substantially larger than the in-place loan of $7,134,251. This large difference implies that there is plenty of additional value that a lender can lend against in order to safely "take out" the existing loan. Furthermore, the DSCR for this new Base Case loan is 1.56x which means there may be additional loan proceeds available if a lender at that point in time is willing to lend above 75% LTV or if market cap rates are below our projected refinance cap rate in the future.

Refinance Exit Test		
Operational Shock	Capital Markets Shock	Both
$679,030	$897,017	$679,030
$11,317,168	$13,000,250	$9,841,015
$8,487,876	$9,750,188	$7,380,762
75%	75%	75%
1.56x	1.46x	1.46x

The Operational Shock is our exit stress test that stresses the revenue of the property but maintains the valuation parameters and interest rate used in the Base Case. As shown before, operational shock reduces revenue by 10%, resulting in a 24.3% drop in NOI. With this lower NOI, the property valuation is lower ($11,317,168 instead of $14,950,288). As a reminder, valuation equals NOI divided by cap rate (we are using a 6% cap rate here). Even though the NOI has endured a hypothetical 24.3% decline, there is still enough value for the new loan to be greater than the existing loan ($8,487,876 > $7,134,251), thus passing this Operational Shock test.

The Capital Markets Shock leaves the operations (NOI) alone and instead stresses the cap rate at which the cash flow is valued while also raising the interest rate (increasing the debt service load, reducing the DSCR). In this example, the cap rate rises from 6% to 6.9% (15% increase) and the refinance loan interest rate rises from 5% to 6.25% (25% increase). Despite the resulting fall in valuation from $14,950,288 to $13,000,250, the new loan is still much larger than the existing loan and the DSCR is sufficient to support the new debt load as well. As you can see, the Capital

Markets Shock was easier to pass than the Operational Shock but this needn't necessarily be the case – the parameters of the stress test could be varied based on your risk tolerance or downside scenarios. To make the stress test more conservative, you could lower LTV as lenders tighten up their underwriting criteria in a Capital Markets Shock-type scenario. However, the unfortunate reality of market cycles is that when operations deteriorate, investor sentiment weakens, which negatively impacts capital markets. Because of this reality, the Both scenario is the worst case scenario but also not terribly unrealistic.

The Both Shock includes falling revenue as well as rising interest rate and cap rate (reducing valuation). As you can see, the Both scenario has a new loan of $7,380,762 which is just slightly greater than the existing loan, thus passing the rigorous Both exit test. Because we assumed the existing loan was a 10-year loan with moderate leverage and only one year of interest-only loan payments, the Both exit test was passable. Nine years of amortization helped reduce the loan balance from $8,550,000 at the start to $7,134,251, making it much easier to refinance out of the loan. Based on these exit tests, we can feel comfortable taking on this combination of leverage and maturity risk for this hypothetical investment. Generally speaking, the longer term the loan is, the lower the maturity risk.

Next, let's keep the underwriting inputs the same, but change the going-in loan to a bridge loan at higher leverage, full-term interest-only payments, and a shorter maturity of only 36 months. All of these factors will certainly make it much harder to pass these exit tests.

Refinance Exit Test Assumptions		
	Inputs	Result
Refi in Month	36	FAIL
Operational Shock	10%	-23.6%
Capital Markets Shock		
Interest Rate Increase	25%	6.25%
Refi Cap Rate Increase	15%	6.90%

In the table above, we changed the Refi in Month input to 36, reflecting the shorter term of the bridge loan. All of the other parameters of this stress test remain the same. The FAIL to the right of "36" is a spoiler alert that this scenario will not end well.

	Current	Base Case
NOI	$810,874	$810,874
Valuation	$13,514,564	$13,514,564
Loan Amount	$9,120,000	$10,135,923
LTV	68.0%	75.0%
DSCR	1.38x	1.56x

Due to the higher going-in leverage as well as the lack of amortization in the loan, the existing loan balance at refinance is $9,120,000, much larger than in our previous scenario ($7,134,251). In this example, only the Base Case passes the exit test with a future loan balance greater than the existing loan balance. This failure in the refinance exit test highlights that a capital call for the difference between the loan amounts would be needed just to pay off the existing mortgage.

Refinance Exit Test		
Operational Shock	Capital Markets Shock	Both
$619,195	$810,874	$619,195
$10,319,924	$11,751,795	$8,973,847
$7,739,943	$8,813,846	$6,730,385
75%	75%	75%
1.56x	1.46x	1.46x

For example, in the Both scenario, there is a $2,389,615 shortfall to be funded by additional capital, either by a capital call for more equity or by subordinate financing, such as a mezzanine loan, should it be available in this downside scenario. This bridge loan example shows the value of the exit test and emphasizes the importance of using appropriate leverage that matches the business plan. I mention the importance of matching the business plan because, as you can see in our example, our hypothetical deal is much better suited for longer term financing at moderate leverage, rather than a short-term high leverage bridge loan. This is the case even though the projected returns are higher in the bridge loan scenario with its higher leverage and quicker sale (realizing the increased value in a shorter period of time). Our example deal has a 19.5% projected IRR for a 3-year bridge loan/3-year sale scenario while the 10-year loan/10-year sale scenario only has a 14.8% IRR. Again, although the higher return opportunity may seem more attractive on the surface, the reality is the opposite, though this is only revealed after further analysis and investigation, including the exit test.

Some might conclude from these results that a bridge loan is bad or risky in all situations, but I would disagree. First, there are some deals for which permanent financing is unavailable and a bridge loan is the only option. More importantly, a bridge loan may be the most efficient capital structure for a given deal if it is a heavy turnaround or includes a large renovation budget, which can be financed by a bridge lender. Nevertheless, because maturity risk comes into play within one to three years on a bridge loan, it is even more important to stress the downside scenarios to see if the bridge loan can be taken out with a refinance or the property can be sold at a high enough price to pay off the lender and preserve equity capital or take a modest loss.

Other Sensitivity Analyses and Risk Metrics

"The market can stay irrational longer than you can stay solvent." —John Maynard Keynes

Thus far we've gone over breakeven occupancy calculations and refinance/exit stress tests, the two most helpful stress tests to analyze both loan default risk and loan maturity risk. Now let's turn to two-way sensitivity tables, which sensitizes the net to investor IRR by changing key metrics. Below is a commonly used two-way table showing how changes in annual rent growth and exit cap rate affect investors' net IRR.

IRR Sensitivity: Terminal Cap Rate Vs Annual Rent Growth								
	Annual Rent Growth							
	1.00%	1.25%	1.50%	1.75%	2.00%	2.25%	2.50%	2.75%
6.75%	6.1%	7.1%	7.7%	8.3%	8.9%	9.5%	10.1%	10.7%
6.50%	7.9%	8.5%	9.2%	9.8%	10.4%	11.0%	11.5%	12.1%
6.25%	9.4%	10.0%	10.7%	11.3%	11.8%	12.4%	13.0%	13.5%
6.00%	11.0%	11.6%	12.2%	12.8%	**13.3%**	13.9%	14.5%	15.0%
5.75%	12.6%	13.2%	13.7%	14.3%	14.9%	15.4%	16.0%	16.5%
5.50%	14.2%	14.8%	15.4%	15.9%	16.5%	17.0%	17.4%	17.9%
5.25%	15.9%	16.4%	17.0%	17.4%	17.9%	18.4%	18.8%	19.3%

(Row labels: Exit Cap Rate)

I like to set up these tables so that projected returns increase from left to right and from top to bottom. Based on our range of inputs, the worst expected outcome is only 6.1% IRR, which is not bad at all for a downside scenario. As an investor, you may want to change the range for annual rent growth and exit cap rate to see how much worse the downside can get. While these tables look fancy and are helpful, they are not the full picture and don't give as much comfort in a downside scenario as the breakeven occupancy and refinance/exit tests. Nevertheless, we can look at a few more examples.

| IRR Sensitivity: Terminal Cap Rate Vs Hold Period | | | | | | | | |
| | Hold Period (Years) | | | | | | | |
Exit Cap Rate	3	4	5	6	7	8	9	10
6.75%	5.0%	7.9%	8.9%	9.6%	9.9%	10.2%	10.3%	10.4%
6.50%	8.4%	9.8%	10.4%	10.7%	10.8%	10.9%	10.9%	10.9%
6.25%	11.2%	11.7%	11.8%	11.8%	11.8%	11.7%	11.5%	11.4%
6.00%	14.1%	13.8%	13.3%	13.0%	12.7%	12.4%	12.2%	12.0%
5.75%	17.0%	15.8%	14.9%	14.2%	13.7%	13.2%	12.9%	12.5%
5.50%	19.6%	17.8%	16.5%	15.4%	14.7%	14.0%	13.5%	13.1%
5.25%	22.4%	19.7%	17.9%	16.7%	15.7%	14.9%	14.3%	13.7%

In this table, the columns are a range of hold periods and the rows are again exit cap rates. In my opinion, this table gives comfort that strong returns can still be achieved even if the property needs to be held longer than originally anticipated. This may not always be the case if the business plan is a quick two-year flip, but the difference between a five-year hold and a ten-year hold is less substantial.

| IRR Sensitivity: Stabilization Time Vs Hold Period | | | | | | | | |
| | Hold Period (Years) | | | | | | | |
Stabilization Time	3	4	5	6	7	8	9	10
27	12.8%	13.0%	12.7%	12.5%	12.3%	12.0%	11.8%	11.7%
26	13.3%	13.3%	12.9%	12.7%	12.4%	12.2%	12.0%	11.8%
25	13.7%	13.5%	13.1%	12.8%	12.5%	12.3%	12.1%	11.9%
24	14.1%	13.8%	13.3%	13.0%	12.7%	12.4%	12.2%	12.0%
23	14.4%	14.0%	13.5%	13.2%	12.8%	12.6%	12.3%	12.1%
22	14.7%	14.3%	13.7%	13.3%	13.0%	12.7%	12.4%	12.2%
21	15.1%	14.5%	13.9%	13.5%	13.1%	12.8%	12.5%	12.3%

In this table, the hold period columns are the same as the previous table but now the rows are the stabilization timeline in months. As you can see, the stabilization time is more important the shorter the hold period is. For a 10-year hold, the difference in total returns is minimal based on the range of stabilization times. Investors often underestimate the time it takes to accomplish the projected business plan so I always recommend stressing this input.

One last small metric to look at is the percentage of the total returns attributed to cash flow versus appreciation. The greater the proportion of returns from cash flow, the more conservative the deal is since cash flow is more predictable and achievable than anticipated appreciation from a capital event. This percentage varies by business plan and hold period. For example, a heavy reposition deal with a projected sale timeline of less than three years, may have zero to little cash flows and this is perfectly fine. However, this increased risk must be recognized and should be compensated for via higher projected returns. Conversely, a 10-year investment horizon could generate up to 80% of returns from cash flow. If you're looking at a 5-year or 10-year investment and the return from cash flow is less than 50% to 60%, then you may want to take a closer look at the assumptions to see if the returns are not being slightly inflated by rosy exit assumptions.

Stress tests and sensitivity analyses are extremely important as a way to take a deeper dive into the underwritten returns and to determine the optimal business plan and capital structure for a given investment. In this chapter, we reviewed breakeven occupancy analysis, refinance/exit test, and two-way sensitivity tables. These are staple analyses which can be used as the building blocks to build one-off analyses specially for a deal or even for a specific investor requesting particular analyses.

PARTNERSHIP STRUCTURES

Investment fee structures nearly always tout "aligned interests" between sponsor and investors. Sponsors will explain how their particular deal structure is best suited to align their interests with investor returns. However, not all "alignments" of interest are created equal and even the traditional private equity structure (acquisition fee, asset management fee, preferred return, and promote) has incentives which can put LPs and GPs at odds.

First, a review of the typical structure: most multifamily deals have an acquisition fee of 1–2% of the purchase price or total capitalization (be sure to understand which amount percentage fees are based on). There is usually an ongoing asset management fee of 1–2% of the property's effective gross income (beware of asset management fees assessed on total invested capital, which could be more than twice as expensive). Finally, sponsored investments will have a promote or carried interest structure which allows the sponsor to receive a percentage of the investment's profits, typically subordinate to a preferred return of 6 to 10%.

Breakdown of Traditional Promote Structure

If the GP successfully executes a value-add business plan, there will be a large paper promote realizable only at sale. In today's yield-starved environment, little ongoing cashflow above typical preferred distributions to LPs remains for the GP, so GPs make little on an investment until a sale unlocks the capital gains. Furthermore, many investors fear a looming recession and so prefer deals with 10-year, fixed-rate debt – often saddled with yield maintenance or defeasance. These punitive prepayment penalties can make it uneconomic to sell a property sooner than 1–2 years before loan maturity or are forced to sell on assumption. Thus, traditional promote structures will always place long-term investors seeking steady yield at odds with sponsors, who make much more from capital gains achieved via a quicker sale. The effect is not only that sponsors want a sale to realize their gains. A GPs' relative share of profits rises with IRR; since the bulk of sale premium is achieved by the initial value-add, sponsors receive the greatest share of total proceeds when the investment is sold sooner. Longer hold periods spread the initial value creation over longer time periods resulting in lower IRR and lower GP share of profits.

Solutions to this misalignment do exist. Lower

preferred returns can allow sponsors to receive meaningful cashflow while holding an investment. Another solution is a promote crystallization, which is a mutually agreed upon valuation that reallocates equity ownership between GP and LP, bringing the GP's share of equity in line with the share of proceeds it would realize at sale but without exiting the investment. This mechanism eliminates the preferred return and promote structure moving forward and allows all parties to equally participate in the future profits of the project. A deep dive on promote crystallizations is outside the scope of this book but check out the articles on our website (www.lscre.com) for more information.

Theoretically, preferred returns protect LPs from underperformance or business failure, relative to the GP. However, a few incentive issues arise from the preferred return. Since LPs get paid first, GPs make relatively little from moderate returns; they gain disproportionately from outperformance. Thus, preferred return hurdles can encourage sponsors to take more risk to try to achieve higher returns and a better payday.

A Preferred return, or "pref", is usually based on levered cash flow; more debt means higher cash flows on a percentage basis, resulting in higher projected promote for the sponsor. This means that debt-averse investors may struggle to find deals which are leveraged to their liking, or find themselves in deals where supplemental financing added two to five years after acquisition leads to significant return of capital, which may be undesirable for long-term, low risk investors. Investors should check the PPM/operating agreements to see if the sponsor is allowed to encumber the property with additional debt post-acquisition. Personally, I am in favor of additional financing and love deals which have strong enough returns to support maximum leverage.

Lastly, the preferred return highly encourages the GP to distribute out all free cash flow to the partnership rather than reinvest it back into the property. This can be very frustrating for a total return investor like myself. Rather than raising an additional million dollars for budgeted improvements, a sponsor could instead take all cash flow generated by the property and use it to fund the renovations. This lowers the investment's effective basis and increases total returns. However, this tactic doesn't fit in a preferred return structure – the sponsor would get so behind on the pref that they would never make any money. I have heard of sponsors that use this method when investing their own money.

Speaking of getting behind on the pref – investors should understand how their preferred return is calculated. The best case is the preferred return is cumulative and compounding. This means that missed pref payments accrue and additional interest (at the pref rate) is added to the accrued balance. Investors should read the fine print to see whether this is the case on deals which they are considering.

Alternative Promote Structures: Better for Investors?

With the difficulties surrounding the preferred return structure, it may be no surprise that a handful of sponsors cite these difficulties to justify eliminating preferred return in exchange for a lower sponsor promote and zero asset management fees. This is pitched as a simpler structure and better alignment of interests, but (in my opinion) is a simple marketing ploy that results in worse economics for investors and a much worse risk-adjusted return profile.

Here is a quick comparison of a traditional structure versus a "no pref, lower promote" structure. As you can see, the traditional structure here is characterized by a 2% acquisition fee, 2% asset management fee, an 8% preferred return, and a 30% promote. Meanwhile, the "No Pref" alternative structure has the same 2% acquisition fee, no asset management fee, no preferred return, and a straight 20% profit split (80% to investors).

Returns Summary					
Total Equity Check	$11,623,705		Enter Investment Size -->		$100,000
Unlevered IRR	9.7%				
Project IRR	18.7%		**Percent**	**Cash Flow**	**Refi/Sale**
Net of Fees Returns		Year 1	8.3%	$8,271	$0
LP IRR	14.1%	Year 2	9.8%	$9,836	$0
LP Avg Cash on Cash	9.2%	Year 3	10.4%	$10,397	$0
LP Annualized Return	15.7%	Year 4	8.6%	$8,564	$0
LP Equity Multiple	1.79x	Year 5	9.0%	$9,005	$132,606
		Year 6	0.0%	$0	$0
Sponsorship Structure		Year 7	0.0%	$0	$0
Acquisition Fee	2.00%	Year 8	0.0%	$0	$0
Asset Management Fee	2.0%	Year 9	0.0%	$0	$0
Preferred Return	8.0%	Year 10	0.0%	$0	$0
Promote	30%	**TOTAL**	**46%**	**$46,074**	**$132,606**

"No Pref" Returns Summary					
Total Equity Check	$11,623,705		Enter Investment Size -->		$100,000
Unlevered IRR	9.7%				
Project IRR	18.7%		Percent	Cash Flow	Refi/Sale
Net of Fees Returns		Year 1	7.3%	$7,314	$0
LP IRR	14.1%	Year 2	9.1%	$9,144	$0
LP Avg Cash on Cash	8.4%	Year 3	9.8%	$9,807	$0
LP Annualized Return	15.9%	Year 4	7.7%	$7,731	$0
LP Equity Multiple	1.80x	Year 5	8.3%	$8,254	$137,264
		Year 6	0.0%	$0	$0
Sponsorship Structure		Year 7	0.0%	$0	$0
Acquisition Fee	2.00%	Year 8	0.0%	$0	$0
Asset Management Fee	0.0%	Year 9	0.0%	$0	$0
Preferred Return	0.0%	Year 10	0.0%	$0	$0
Promote	20%	**TOTAL**	**42%**	**$42,250**	**$137,264**

Oddly enough, between these two scenarios, in this particular situation, investor IRRs are the same but cash flows in the "No Pref" are almost 100 basis points lower. Furthermore, investors are at a substantially higher risk of underperformance in the latter structure because they are not protected by a preferred return. For example, here are the returns for the same deal with vacancy stressed from 7% to 12%.

Returns Summary					
Total Equity Check	$11,622,435		Enter Investment Size -->		$100,000
Unlevered IRR	7.3%				
Project IRR	12.0%		Percent	Cash Flow	Refi/Sale
Net of Fees Returns		Year 1	6.5%	$6,497	$0
LP IRR	9.5%	Year 2	8.6%	$8,643	$0
LP Avg Cash on Cash	7.7%	Year 3	9.2%	$9,225	$0
LP Annualized Return	9.9%	Year 4	6.7%	$6,704	$0
LP Equity Multiple	1.49x	Year 5	7.3%	$7,275	$109,075
		Year 6	0.0%	$0	$0
Sponsorship Structure		Year 7	0.0%	$0	$0
Acquisition Fee	2.00%	Year 8	0.0%	$0	$0
Asset Management Fee	2.0%	Year 9	0.0%	$0	$0
Preferred Return	8.0%	Year 10	0.0%	$0	$0
Promote	30%	**TOTAL**	**38%**	**$38,344**	**$109,075**

"No Pref" Returns Summary					
Total Equity Check	$11,622,435		Enter Investment Size -->		$100,000
Unlevered IRR	7.3%				
Project IRR	12.0%		Percent	Cash Flow	Refi/Sale
Net of Fees Returns		Year 1	5.8%	$5,770	$0
LP IRR	8.5%	Year 2	7.5%	$7,527	$0
LP Avg Cash on Cash	6.8%	Year 3	8.1%	$8,138	$0
LP Annualized Return	8.9%	Year 4	6.0%	$6,013	$0
LP Equity Multiple	1.44x	Year 5	6.5%	$6,488	$110,372
		Year 6	0.0%	$0	$0
Sponsorship Structure		Year 7	0.0%	$0	$0
Acquisition Fee	2.00%	Year 8	0.0%	$0	$0
Asset Management Fee	0.0%	Year 9	0.0%	$0	$0
Preferred Return	0.0%	Year 10	0.0%	$0	$0
Promote	20%	**TOTAL**	**34%**	**$33,936**	**$110,372**

In this case, both investor IRRs were at 14.1% and are hit by the increase in vacancy but the traditional structure held up better to the stress test because the preferred return was caught up by profits from the sale. Without a preferred return, investors have full exposure to the ups and downs of the investment's performance. In conclusion, a cumulative and compounding preferred return is almost always optimal for investor economics and is a great alignment of interest when employed properly.

We are not, however, in the clear yet. A nefarious and return-dilutive strategy exists whereby the sponsor "over-raises" enough equity from investors prior to closing to pay any shortfalls in the preferred return. This is fantastic marketing because the sponsor can still include a pref in their structure yet know they can reach into the cookie jar for their promote at will because they have the power to always stay current on their pref.

As an aside, this makes sponsors like us who don't play this game look extremely bad when we don't meet our pref in the first year or two. Investor: "Why can't you pay my pref when the sponsor down the street just paid a 4 cap and is paying out 8%?" *Magic… Or* – they are using *your* money to pay *your* return so they can earn their promote sooner.

This strategy is the opposite of reinvesting cash flows to be more capital efficient and achieve a lower basis. Instead, pre-raising the pref increases the total amount of equity required to make the investment which dilutes total returns and sale profits across a larger equity slice. **Worse still, this has no effect on the sponsor's sale compensation – the sponsor earns a fixed percentage of the sale profits regardless of how much equity there is to split it with.** "Over-raising" or "pre-raising the pref" not only lowers investors returns, it also eliminates the preferred return's power as an alignment of interest, rendering it inert.

Hidden Fees

Additional ancillary or hidden fees don't necessarily bring interests into or out of alignment, but are important to recognize and reflect the sponsor's approach to business. The largest and most-overlooked fee is the loan guarantee fee, which can sometimes be lost in the laundry list of fees associated with financing. There are often numerous parties receiving fees in the financing process so it is worth understanding who exactly gets what. Sponsors sometimes assess a guarantee fee on the loan balance for signing on the loan – I would argue this is justified for recourse debt with below-market terms such as a low interest rate. It would be well worth it for an investor to pay a 1% loan guarantee fee to a sponsor who signs a recourse loan with an interest rate that is 50 bps below market.

However, assessing a guarantee fee on a non-recourse loan is a fee grab – a sign of a sponsor seeking to maximize the upfront fees they receive. Other "hidden fees" include expenses charged to the property that really ought to be covered by the sponsor or management company. Asset management fees are paid to "keep the lights on" and cover such costs. However, some sponsors charge travel costs to the property and I've even been told by a sponsor that he bills his properties his hourly rate when on site. All this begs the question – if this is happening in plain sight, what is being charged/manipulated behind the scenes? I encourage investors to ask sponsors which costs are/are not covered by the asset management fee.

Lastly, I would like to touch on creative structures. We analyzed the "no pref" structure – pitched as more investor-friendly but shown to be more expensive with a worse risk profile. Sadly, most creative structures are more of the same. Sponsors will typically diverge from the traditional structure because they believe it will pay them better. We are always analyzing unique structures in the market and working to devise new structures that are a win/wins for the GP and LP, such as not taking an acquisition fee, preferred equity, dual-tranche syndication, and promote crystallization.

So, what solution is there when so many structures fail to deliver favorable post-fee economics or properly align interests? The truest alignment of interest is GP co-investment. Cash (co-invested) is king. The best structure is one that includes the sponsor investing significant cash (relative to their net worth), net of all upfront fees and on the same terms as LPs. This is very rare and can be difficult, especially for newer sponsors who may not have the luxury of investing much at all. When substantial co-invest isn't feasible, investors should ensure that newer sponsors are long-term oriented and are invested in their reputations. Investment by family members of the sponsor may also carry similar weight. In conclusion, investors should underwrite every deal they consider, fully understand the nuances of proposed deal structures, and be aware of GP co-investment and hidden fees.

The incorporation of partnership structures and profit splits usually manifest themselves in underwriting models via a waterfall module. As both a sponsor or investor in real estate partnerships, it is helpful to understand and be able to build waterfall structures. Waterfalls are the way profits flow through a partnership.

We touched upon the basics of waterfalls by explaining the way preferred returns/IRR hurdles and promotes/carried interests work. A waterfall is the best way to actually model out these partnership terms in a spreadsheet. The project-level cash flows start at the top of the waterfall and then flow through multiple tiers.

For example, the first tier is usually a preferred return, meaning investors are entitled to 100% of the returns up to that return threshold. Above the preferred return hurdle, the sponsor begins to participate in the profits. Additionally, there can be subsequent tiers, or higher return hurdles which increase the sponsor's compensation.

Here is an example of a multi-tiered partnership structure (please note that having this many tiers is not very common nor a great idea; I believe keeping things as simple as possible is usually the best protocol).

Promote Structure		
Tier	Hurdle	Promote
Tier 1/Preferred Return	7%	0%
Tier 2	15%	20%
Tier 3	18%	30%
Tier 4	18%	40%

This example has a 7% preferred return and as described, the promote up to 7% is 0% – defining this tier as a preferred obligation to investors. Subsequently, the sponsor is entitled to 20% of the profits above 7%, up to 15%. Above a 15% IRR, the sponsor now receives 30% of profits up to 18%. Finally, for any profits above an 18% IRR, the sponsor receives 40%.

For the majority of investments, it is unlikely to achieve 18% returns, which is another reason why I don't think it is a great idea to have a complex, multi-tiered structure, since they are unlikely to come into play at this late stage of the market cycle when prospective returns are low. Additionally, a lower secondary hurdle of around 13% is uncompetitive and sophisticated investors will rightfully "throw up over it". Investors sometimes neglect to ask about this feature, which is unlikely to be front-and-center in investment summaries or presentations.

A tier 2 hurdle should be a step below a "home run hurdle," but should not be set so low as to be very easy to achieve. This means that a tier 2 hurdle rate should be based on 1) market rate for multiple-level promote structures and 2) projected returns of a particular project. For example, a fairly conservative value-add deal, with projected returns of 16%, could reasonably structure a tier 2 hurdle entitling the sponsor to 50% of the profits above an 18% IRR. This is because an 18% IRR is a terrific risk-adjusted return and above what the sponsor is reasonably projecting to achieve. Conversely, a 13% tier 2 hurdle rate would be unfair to investors since the hurdle may well be reached and dampen investor returns in a moderate upside scenario.

Another wrinkle is whether sponsor begins receiving the higher tier 2 promote share when *the project* reaches the tier 2 hurdle IRR, or when *investors* receive that rate. Of course, investors would want this threshold to be based on net returns – which is typical, but not always the case. Investors, for all deals and deal structures, should sensitize their net returns to see how a deal's structure affects their economics in both upside and downside scenarios.

A preferred return and a secondary hurdle can be appropriate depending on the deal but investors should recognize that a secondary hurdle which increases sponsor returns will incentivize the sponsor to take more risk and sell sooner in order to try to maximize the project's IRR to hit their higher promote hurdle. For shorter-term, heavier turnaround business plans, this structure can make sense because it aligns the interests of the sponsor and investors to execute the business plan as quickly and effectively as possible.

Promote structures should benefit investors by aligning the interests of GP and LP and incentivizing the GP to create outsized returns. Many investors, though, are wary of structures that encourage sponsors to seek risk in order to maximize pay. At the end of the day, the single strongest aligner of interests is cash out-of-pocket invested by the sponsor on the same terms as limited partners.

Preferred returns and promote structures are not all created equal (even if the numbers look the same). Two deals could both have an 8% preferred return and a 30% promote, but work differently in ways that meaningfully impact returns to investors. For example, preferred returns can be compounding or not, and the rate at which it compounds can vary. Additionally, a sponsor catch-up could follow once the preferred return is paid. A catch up is triggered after LPs are paid out their preferred return and pays all remaining cash flow above the pref to the sponsor until the ratio of distributions balances out to the promote split. This provision is often under-explained and not always well enough understood – "GP catch-up" structures can be costly and reduce investor returns more than expected.

A preferred return can also be implemented more like an IRR hurdle rate, changing the cash flows investors receive throughout the hold period of a cash flowing investment. An IRR hurdle structure subordinates sponsors' promote not only to the hurdle rate but also to a 100% return of investor capital. This way, investors are promised a certain compounding rate of return including full return of capital before sponsor receives any promote compensation. This is the standard, institutional definition of a preferred return hurdle.

This IRR-hurdle type of preferred return is rare in widely syndicated multifamily deals, since investors are often unaware of it, and sponsors usually command terms. The common syndication structure sees the sponsor collecting promote on ongoing cash flows that exceed the preferred return rate. This arrangement is frowned upon by institutional investors, since a sponsor could collect a promote in a year of strong cash flows (or simply due to interest-only loan payments) then underperform the next year (or amortize) – while suffering neither penalty nor clawback of the previous year's promote compensation.

In fairness, it is rare in today's low-return environment to find investment opportunities with projected cash flows much above the preferred return rate, so ongoing cashflow promote in most deals is minimal. However, the ongoing cashflow preferred rate structure seen in syndications can be especially pernicious when a sponsor "pre-raises capital" to meet their cashflow distribution requirements. The sponsor is then assured promote on cashflow since preferred distributions are a certainty (paid from the "pre-raised" capital). Still more dishonest, some sponsors then tout an asset management fee subordinate to the preferred return – a low risk move when the preferred return is paid out of pre-raised capital (how can we compete with that!?).

Yes, I have been asked by an investor if our asset management fee is subordinate to the "pref" and was looked upon negatively when I of course conceded it is not. This all goes to say that the desirability of a preferred return isn't as simple as just the percentage rate – details matter and must be fully understood in order to accurately underwrite net returns to investors.

All of these various components to a joint venture structure can be complex and difficult to calculate by hand or from a blank spreadsheet, which is often required for more esoteric wrinkles. The standard method to calculate preferred returns and promotes is via a waterfall model – either a standalone workbook or built onto a discounted cash flow or underwriting model.

Fortunately, I've built a waterfall module in our underwriting model which allows for easy evaluation of net returns to investors and their various components to determine optimal structure from both a GP and LP perspective. Both sponsors and investors would be well served to fully understand the structures they are creating and investing in.

To that end, in our underwriting model, I've created a section which analyzes the sponsor's compensation. The best way to calculate sponsor compensation is as a percentage of equity required to raise to complete the deal. It wouldn't be fair to compare a $1,000,000 deal and a $100,000,000 in gross dollar terms. Next, it isn't fair to compare the total compensation from a 3-year investment and a 10-year investment, since the 10-year hold will result in higher fees collected in total. To combat this discrepancy, compensation should be evaluated on a net present value (NPV) basis. This means that money received in the future is appropriately discounted back to present value in order to compare apples-to-apples.

Below in the table, you can see I've chosen 20% as the discount rate for the NPV calculation. For reference, to the right of the 20% input, I've included the net levered IRR for the project as it may be appropriate to adjust the discount rate based on the return projection for the investment.

Sponsor Compensation Analysis		
NPV Calculation Discount Rate	20.0%	13.6%
Promote Uncertainty Discount	30.0%	27.1%
	Nominal	**NPV**
Total Sponsor Compensation	$1,279,504	$386,727
Total / Equity Raised	36.0%	10.9%
Total Fee Compensation	$495,491	$260,105
Total Performance Compensation	$784,013	$126,622
Uncertainty Discounted	$548,809	$88,636
Fee + Uncertainty Discounted	$1,044,300	$348,740
Fee + Uncertainty / Equity Raised	**29.4%**	**9.8%**

Next, I also need to treat performance compensation differently than fee compensation, since performance compensation is far more speculative and at-risk than fee income. Here, I'm using a 30% discount of the promote to account for this. For reference, to the right of the 30% input, I'm showing double the net levered return for the project as a potential proxy for an appropriate discount since the higher the projected returns are, the more risk there is in not achieving them and thus missing on the promote expectation.

Once you have these appropriate NPV and uncertainty discounts assessed to the stream of sponsor fees and promote compensation, a total "Fee + Uncertainty Discounted" compensation can be calculated on an NPV basis.

Lastly, this number ($348,740) can be divided by the amount of equity required for the investment to come up with a final percentage compensation (9.8%). To summarize the meaning of this final percentage, it is the value of the sponsor's compensation in today's terms, discounted for uncertainty, for every dollar raised. In our example, this means for every dollar the sponsor raises, the sponsor is projected to receive 9.8 cents. I recommend sponsors not just evaluate project-level returns or the returns for their investors, but also understand what their compensation is and have some minimum threshold of compensation for pursuing a new deal.

CONCLUSION

We have successfully walked through the complete underwriting process, including gathering the right information, inputting historical financials and future assumptions, verifying assumptions with rental and sales comparables, and stressing/analyzing the results.

We've also taken a deep dive into real estate partnership structures and how to ensure you're investing in a structure that is favorable for you, regardless of which side of the table you sit on. I have great passion for underwriting and am always striving to sharpen my analysts' and my own skills. We are always sharing notes and looking for ways to get more accurate in our underwriting and more insightful with our analysis.

I hope you have found this content useful and mildly entertaining. As I've said many times on podcasts and in this book, I think it is paramount for investors to underwrite every deal they contemplate investing in. Learning about the market and prospective returns is best done through underwriting practice and repetition. I hope you use these tools to make better investment decisions by analyzing project-level returns as well as partnership structures. The better you know the numbers, the better you are able to negotiate the optimal structure based on the unique attributes of the deal and goals of the individual participants of the deal.

Don't hesitate to reach out to me if you are looking for help identifying the best opportunities for yourself or with negotiating the best debt and equity structure for your next deal. Additionally, if you're interested in participating in one of our future investments, make sure you go to our website at www.lscre.com and sign up for our newsletter so you don't miss the next opportunity.

ABOUT THE AUTHOR

 Rob oversees acquisitions and capital markets for Lone Star Capital and has acquired over $350M of multifamily real estate. He has evaluated thousands of opportunities using proprietary underwriting models and published the number one book on multifamily underwriting, The Definitive Guide to Underwriting Multifamily Acquisitions. He has written over 50 articles about underwriting, deal structures, and capital markets and hosts the Capital Spotlight podcast, which is focused on interviewing institutional investors.

★ Lone Star Capital

About Lone Star Capital

Lone Star Capital is a real estate investment firm focused on underperforming multifamily properties in Texas. Lone Star creates core-plus and value-add opportunities that deliver superior risk-adjusted returns by implementing moderate to extensive renovations, improving management, and designing creative capital solutions. Lone Star owns over 2,500 units worth more than $350M.

We Seek Opportunity

Lone Star Capital acquires B/C multifamily properties in Texas and throughout the Southeast. We seek *true* value-add opportunities that are under-managed, have high vacancy, below market rents, and deferred maintenance. We underwrite quickly and make prompt, confident offers. Please reach out if you have an opportunity you believe would be a good fit for us.

Work with Us

We are always looking to build new relationships with equity partners and Co-GPs. Reach out to ir@lscre.com if you would like to discuss our current pipeline of deals and how we may best work together.

Made in the USA
Las Vegas, NV
09 July 2024

92029889R00066